C.I.R. v. Milwaukee & Suburban Transport Corp. U.S. Supreme Court Transcript of Record with Supporting Pleadings

ARCHIBALD COX, ROBERT THORSEN

C.I.R. v. Milwaukee & Suburban Transport Corp.
Petition / ARCHIBALD COX / 1960 / 843 / 367 U.S. 906 / 81 S.Ct. 1917 / 6 L.Ed.2d 1249 / 3-23-1961
C.I.R. v. Milwaukee & Suburban Transport Corp.
Brief in Opposition (P) / ROBERT THORSEN / 1960 / 843 / 367 U.S. 906 / 81 S.Ct. 1917 / 6 L.Ed.2d 1249 / 4-21-1961

C.I.R. v. Milwaukee & Suburban Transport Corp. U.S. Supreme Court Transcript of Record with Supporting Pleadings

Table of Contents

No. — **843**

In the Supreme Court of the United States

OCTOBER TERM, 1960

COMMISSIONER OF INTERNAL REVENUE, PETITIONER

v.

MILWAUKEE & SUBURBAN TRANSPORT CORPORATION

*PETITION FOR A WRIT OF CERTIORARI TO THE UNITED STATES
COURT OF APPEALS FOR THE SEVENTH CIRCUIT*

455

ARCHIBALD COX,
Solicitor General,
LOUIS F. OBERDORFER,
Assistant Attorney General,
HARRY BAUM,
JOSEPH KOVNER,
Attorneys,
Department of Justice, Washington 25, D.C.

INDEX

CITATIONS

(I)

Miscellaneous—Continued

In the Supreme Court of the United States

October Term, 1960

No. —

COMMISSIONER OF INTERNAL REVENUE, PETITIONER

v.

MILWAUKEE & SUBURBAN TRANSPORT CORPORATION

PETITION FOR A WRIT OF CERTIORARI TO THE UNITED STATES COURT OF APPEALS FOR THE SEVENTH CIRCUIT

The Solicitor General, on behalf of the Commissioner of Internal Revenue, petitions for a writ of certiorari to review the judgment of the Court of Appeals for the Seventh Circuit in this case.

OPINIONS BELOW

The memorandum opinion of the Tax Court (Appendix A, *infra*, pp. 10–41) is not officially reported. The opinion of the Court of Appeals (Appendix A, *infra*, pp. 42–60) is reported at 283 F. 2d 279.

JURISDICTION

The judgment of the Court of Appeals was entered on October 24, 1960. (Appendix A, *infra*, pp. 60–61.) The time for filing a petition for a writ of certiorari was extended, by order of Mr. Justice Clark, to and

including March 24, 1961. The jurisdiction of this
Court is invoked under 28 U.S.C., Section 1254(1).

QUESTION PRESENTED

Whether the taxpayer, a municipal transit company filing its federal income tax returns on the
calendar year and accrual basis, may deduct from its
gross income for the taxable years a reserve set up on
its books to reflect estimated amounts of liability for
contested and unsettled claims for personal injuries
and property damages arising out of accidents
occurring in the taxable years.

STATUTES AND REGULATIONS INVOLVED

The pertinent provisions of Sections 22, 23, 41, 42
and 43 of the Internal Revenue Code of 1939 and of
Sections 39.41–1, 39.41–2, 39.42–1, 39.43–1 and 39.43–2
of Treasury Regulations 118 (1939 Code) are
reprinted in Appendix B, *infra,* pp. 61–66.

STATEMENT

The taxpayer, a Wisconsin corporation, operates a
public transportation system and files its returns on a
calendar year and accrual basis. During the taxable
years 1953 and 1954, it operated approximately 1,000
vehicles, carrying from 250,000,000 to 281,000,000
million passengers. In 1953, its vehicles were
involved in 5,903 accidents, and in 1954, there were
5,041 accidents. (Appendix A, *infra,* pp. 30, 50–51.)

The taxpayer was insured for liability, occasioned
by any one accident, in excess of $100,000 and less
than $1,000,000, but was a self-insurer for other lia-

bility. It maintained a staff of attorneys and claims adjusters to investigate, settle and defend claims for personal injuries and property damages. (Appendix A, *infra*, pp. 30–31, 51.)

As of December 31, 1953, there were 414 unsettled claims growing out of accidents occurring in that year; and there were 447 unsettled claims at the end of 1954 arising out of accidents in that year. (Appendix A, *infra*, pp. 31, 51.)

At the end of each year, the information at hand with respect to each of these claims was reviewed by a committee of three members of the taxpayer's executive board, aided by its claim staff. The committee made an appraisal or estimate of the amount for which, in their opinion, the taxpayer was liable, if at all, in each instance, and authorized the general claim agent to dispose of the claims at the appraised amounts. Its action was ratified by the board of directors. (Appendix A, *infra*, pp. 31–32, 51–52.)

The total estimated amount was set up on the taxpayer's books of account as a book liability for unsettled claims for injuries and damages. This amount was $254,659 for 1953 and $161,136.50 in 1954. (Appendix A, *infra*, pp. 32, 52.)

Liability as to all claims was actively contested by the taxpayer. It denied liability on a claim when filed, and pleaded no liability on claims in suit. Suit had been brought on 22 claims in 1953, and on 16 claims in 1954. In addition, and included in the estimate for each year, were a number of instances in which no claim had yet been filed. The appraised estimates were kept confidential and the taxpayer's agents in fact tried to settle claims at the lowest possible figure. (Appendix A, *infra,* pp. 33–34, 52.)

The estimates varied greatly from actual settlements in nearly all of the particular claims, and the total estimate for each year varied substantially from the total amount eventually paid on the claims. (Appendix A, *infra,* pp. 38–39, 53.) Thus, the estimate was the same as the amount actually paid in only 10 percent of the claims (31 out of 261 in 1953, 22 out of 254 in 1954), while the estimates varied from actual payments by more than 100 percent in 40 percent of the claims (97 in 1953 and 102 in 1954). (Appendix A, *infra,* pp. 34–35, 51.) Many other settlements varied more than 50 percent from the estimates of liability. In over 90 percent of the cases in which the company had originally estimated it had no liability, it actually did make a monetary settlement. (Appendix A, *infra,* p. 39.) At the time of the trial below (August, 1958), there were still some unsettled claims as to which the original estimates of liability had been substantially revised. (Appendix A, *infra,* pp. 35, 53.)[1]

The original estimate of liability for 1953 reflected in the reserve account exceeded the total of the actual liability (actual settlements plus currently revised estimates of unsettled claims) by over 32 percent. On the other hand, the original estimate of liability

---

[1] Thus, "As of the time of trial, there were still 8 unsettled 1953 claims where liability was currently estimated at $14,500, although the original estimate was $5,200. In addition, there were 13 unsettled 1954 claims currently estimated at $51,415 and originally estimated at $12,750." (Appendix A, *infra,* p. 53.)

for 1954 turned out to be some 31 percent less than the actual liability.[2]

In its tax return for 1953, the taxpayer deducted as an expense for that year the sum of $254,659, representing its estimated amount of liability on unsettled claims arising out of accidents occurring in that year. In its return for 1954, it claimed a deduction of $142,022, representing its estimated amount of liability on account of 1954 accidents ($161,136), reduced by the difference between its estimated amount of liability on 1953 claims settled in 1954 ($94,984) and the amounts at which such claims were actually settled ($75,870). The Commissioner allowed as a deduction in each year only the amount of claims which were actually settled in that year. (Appendix A, *infra*, pp. 32–33.) The Tax Court sustained the Commissioner's determination. (Appendix A, *infra*, pp. 36–41.) The Court of Appeals reversed. (Appendix A, *infra*, pp. 50–60.)

REASONS FOR GRANTING THE WRIT

We believe that the decision below is incorrect and that it is contrary to decisions of this and other courts.

---

[2] A comparison of the taxpayer's aggregate estimates with actual settlement figures for the years 1953 and 1954 follows (Appendix A, *infra*, p. 58):

1953 Estimate—$254,659.00

Cost of 1953 cases settled	$178,230.24
Current estimate of unsettled cases	14,500.00
Total	192,730.24

1954 Estimate—$161,136.50

Cost of 1954 cases settled	159,851.84
Current estimate of unsettled cases	51,415.00
Total	211,266.84

However, since the question presented is related to those involved in two cases awaiting argument in this Court (*American Automobile Assn.* v. *United States*, No. 288; *United States* v. *Consolidated Edison Co. of New York*, No. 357) and several others in which petitions for certiorari are pending (*New Jersey Automobile Club* v. *United States*, No. 140; *Streight Radio and Television, Inc.* v. *Commissioner*, No. 507; *Commissioner* v. *Schlude*, No. 629; *Fifth Avenue Coach Lines, Inc.* v. *Commissioner*, No. 634), the Court may wish to defer action on this petition pending its decision in the *American Automobile Assn.* and *Consolidated Edison* cases.[3]

1. The taxpayer, a common carrier filing its returns on the calendar year and accrual basis, set up on its books a reserve account to reflect estimated amounts of contingent liabilities for contested and unsettled personal injury and property damage claims arising out of the operation of its transportation facilities, and in its returns for the taxable years (1953 and 1954) it deducted such amounts in computing its net income subject to federal income tax. The Tax Court held that the estimated amounts reflected in the reserve account were not accruable and deductible in the respective taxable years in which they were claimed as deductions, since the taxpayer's liability to pay had not become definite but, on the contrary, was being contested. The court below reversed on the

---

[3] The petitions for certiorari in *New Jersey Automobile Club*, *Streight Radio*, *Schlude*, and *Fifth Avenue Coach Lines* are apparently being held to await the disposition of the *American Automobile Assn.* and *Consolidated Edison* cases.

theory that, although the taxpayer's liability for each individual claim was being contested and remained contingent, the "aggregate" amount of "over-all" liability could be "accurately predicted." In so holding the court below violated the settled annual accounting rule, and the equally settled corollary principle that an item of deduction (expense, loss, etc.) is accruable as an offset against gross income only in the taxable year in which the liability to pay it becomes fixed, in *fact* as well as in *amount*. *Security Mills Co.* v. *Commissioner*, 321 U.S. 281; *Dixie Pine Co.* v. *Commissioner*, 320 U.S. 516; *Brown* v. *Helvering*, 291 U.S. 193; *Lucas* v. *American Code Co.*, 280 U.S. 445; *United States* v. *Anderson*, 269 U.S. 422.

2. The decision below is also in conflict with decisions of other Courts of Appeals. *E.g., Spring Canyon Coal Co.* v. *Commissioner*, 43 F. 2d 78 (C.A. 10th), certiorari denied, 284 U.S. 654; *United States* v. *Texas Mexican Railway Co.*, 263 F. 2d 31 (C.A. 5th); *Capital Warehouse Co.* v. *Commissioner*, 171 F. 2d 395 (C.A. 8th); *Spencer, White & Prentis* v. *Commissioner*, 144 F. 2d 45 (C.A. 2d), certiorari denied, 323 U.S. 780. See, also, *Commissioner* v. *Fifth Avenue Coach Lines*, 281 F. 2d 556 (C.A. 2d), pending on the taxpayer's petition for certiorari (No. 634). Indeed, it is contrary to the Seventh Circuit's own prior decision in *Streight Radio and Television, Inc.* v. *Commissioner*, 280 F. 2d 883, pending on the taxpayer's petition for certiorari (No. 507).[4]

---

[4] The court's reliance upon *Ocean Accident & G. Corp.* v. *Commissioner*, 47 F. 2d 582 (C.A. 2d), was patently misplaced. That case involved the computation of taxable income of an "insurance company," governed by special provisions of the

3. Furthermore, the decision below attempts to reinstate an exception to the annual accounting rule which Congress has authoritatively rejected. Section 462 of the 1954 Code (26 U.S.C. 1952 ed., Supp. II, Sec. 462) authorized a deduction by accrual basis taxpayers of a reasonable "reserve for estimated expenses." The House and Senate Committee Reports indicated that its purpose was, among others, to allow a deduction for estimated amounts of "certain liabilities for self-insured injury and damage claims." H. Rep. No. 1337, 83d Cong., 2d Sess., p. A163 (3 U.S.C. Cong. & Adm. News (1954) 4017, 4301); S. Rep. No. 1622, 83d Cong., 2d Sess., pp. 63, 305–307 (3 U.S.C. Cong. & Adm. News (1954) 4621, 4695, 4945–4947). The repeal of the section shortly after its enactment (Act of June 15, 1955, c. 143, 69 Stat. 134, Sec. 1) withdrew the authorization for such a deduction, over the protests of witnesses for the transportation industry. See House Hearings, Prepaid Income and Reserves for Estimated Expenses, on H.R. 4725, 84th Cong., 1st Sess., pp. 153–154, 156, 188–189; Senate Hearings, p. 67. The court below has in effect applied a statute which Congress had repealed.

Internal Revenue Code applicable to such companies. See 1939 Code Section 204(b) (6) and (7), (c) (1) and (4); 1954 Code Section 832(b) (5) and (6), (c) (1) and (4); *Spring Canyon Coal Co. v. Commissioner, supra; Richmond Light & Railroad Co. v. Commissioner,* 4 B.T.A. 91; O. D. 879, 4 Cum. Bull. 142 (1921).

CONCLUSION

For the reasons stated, this case merits review. We recognize, however, that the Court may wish to withhold action upon the petition pending its disposition of the *American Automobile Assn.* and *Consolidated Edison* cases (Nos. 288 and 357).

Respectfully submitted.

ARCHIBALD COX,
Solicitor General.
LOUIS F. OBERDORFER,
Assistant Attorney General.
HARRY BAUM,
JOSEPH KOVNER,
Attorneys.

MARCH 1961.

APPENDIX A

Opinion

T. C. Memo. 1959–216

TAX COURT OF THE UNITED STATES

Milwaukee & Suburban Transport Corporation, Petitioner *vs.* Commissioner of Internal Revenue, Respondent

Docket Nos. 61395, 72017. Filed November 18, 1959

1. Petitioner paid certain amounts as dividends on its preferred stock, issued in connection with its purchase of the mass public passenger transportation system in the City of Milwaukee from a corporation which was compelled to divest itself of the same in order to comply with the provisions of the Public Utility Holding Company Act of 1935. Held: Said dividends are not deductible as "interest on indebtedness," within the meaning of section 23(b) of the 1939 Code and section 163(a) of the 1954 Code, inasmuch as the preferred stock represented an equity investment and not a debt.

2. Petitioner kept its books of account on an accrual basis. At the end of each of its first two taxable years, 1953 and 1954, it estimated its liability for potential and unsettled property damage and personal injury claims, arising out of accidents in which its employees and equipment were involved. And although it denied any liability to the injured parties, it accrued on its books of account as a liability, and charged to expense, the amount of such estimates;

and it deducted the same on its Federal income tax
returns.   Held: The amounts of such estimated
espenses were not accruable and also not deductible
for tax purposes, for the reasons that, as of the close
of each taxable year, (1) petitioner's liability for said
potential and unsettled claims was not definitely
fixed; and (2) the amount of any liability which it
might have, could not be ascertained with reasonable
certainty.

Richard R. Teschner, Esq., Dale L. Sorden, Esq.,
J. Roy Browning, Esq., W. W. Browning, Esq., and
Robert Thorsen, Esq., for the petitioner.

Thomas J. Donnelly, Jr., Esq., for the respondent.

MEMORANDUM FINDINGS OF FACT AND OPINION

PIERCE, *Judge*.

The respondent determined deficiencies in the petitioner's income taxes in the amounts of $209,233.75
and $110,094.67 for the taxable years 1953 and 1954,
respectively.

The two cases were consolidated for trial.

The issues presented for decision are:

(1) Whether certain amounts which petitioner paid as "dividends" on securities designated as preferred stock were, in substance
and reality, "interest on indebtedness," so as to
be deductible from gross income under section
23(b) of the 1939 Code and section 163(a) of
the 1954 Code. Incidental to this issue are
the further questions of whether petitioner is
entitled to deduct in each of the taxable years,
a pro rata portion of the expense of issuing
said securities; and whether it also is entitled
to deduct for the first of said years, a net
operating loss carryover deduction from the
prior year, which was based on deductions for
said expense of issuing the securities, and for
claimed "interest" thereon.

(2) Whether petitioner properly accrued on its books of account and deducted on its Federal income tax return for each of the taxable years, its estimated amount of liabilities for personal injury and property damages alleged to have been sustained in accidents in which petitioner's employees were involved, where the claims for such damages were unsettled and contested at the close of each of the taxable years.

Some of the facts were stipulated. The stipulation of facts, together with the exhibits attached thereto and identified therein, is incorporated herein by reference.

I.   Issue re Interest Deduction

Findings of Fact

Petitioner is a corporation organized on October 7, 1952, under the laws of the State of Wisconsin. It filed its returns for the taxable years 1953 and 1954 with the director of internal revenue for the district of Wisconsin. It kept its books of account and filed its Federal income tax returns in accordance with an accrual method of accounting and on the basis of calendar years.

Petitioner was originally incorporated under the name of Harbor Transportation Corporation. Shortly thereafter, it changed its name to Milwaukee & Suburban Transport Corporation, which it has since continued to use. At the time of its organization, petitioner's total capital was $1,000, represented by 10 shares of common capital stock of the par value of $100 per share.

In the year 1952, and for several years prior thereto, the public passenger transportation system in the City of Milwaukee and its environs was owned and operated by the Milwaukee Electric Railway and Transport Company (hereinafter called the Transport Company) which was a wholly-owned subsidiary of the Wisconsin Electric Power Company (hereinafter called the Power Company). Both the parent and the subsidiary were Wisconsin corporations; and the parent also was a registered public utility holding company, subject to the provisions of the Federal Public Utility Holding Company Act of 1935 (Title 15 U.S.C., section 79).

During the 1940's, the management of the Power Company and of the Transport Company came to realize that by reason of the provisions of the Public Utility Holding Company Act of 1935, it would be necessary to remove the public passenger transportation properties owned by the subsidiary Transport Company, from the holding company system of the parent Power Company. Looking to that end, the management of the two companies undertook extended efforts to find a purchaser for said properties. In 1947, a prospectus offering the properties for sale was issued and widely distributed; but no bids were received. Between 1947 and 1952, negotiations were had with approximately 10 different groups of possible purchasers, including the City of Milwaukee; but the only firm offer received was that of a group made up of four individuals who ultimately became the incorporators and common stockholders of the petitioner corporation.

The negotiations between the above-mentioned group and the Transport Company began in the summer of 1950; and by the summer of 1952, general agreement between the parties had been reached on the terms of the proposed sale of the Transport Company's transportation properties. The purchase price

finally agreed upon was $10,000,000, payable in the
following manner: $4,000,000 in cash, to be raised by
a purchasing corporation to be organized (i.e., the
petitioner) which would float bonds to outside parties,
secured by a first mortgage on the assets to be purchased; $3,000,000 of the purchasing corporation's
promissory notes, which were to be issued to the
Transport Company, and which were to be secured by
a second mortgage on such assets; and $3,000,000 in
preferred stock to be issued to the Transport Company. Also, the four individuals were to invest an
aggregate of $500,000 cash in common stock of the
corporation to be formed, in order to supply working
capital. In adopting such plan, it was the belief of
the parties that, if the issuance of the securities by
the purchasing corporation was to receive the
required approval of the Public Service Commission
of Wisconsin (hereinafter called the P.S.C.), the
ratio of corporate debt to equity capital could not be
too high. Also it was believed that, if the sale was to
receive the required approval of the United States
Securities and Exchange Commission (hereinafter
called the S.E.C.) as a divestiture by the Power Company of the public passenger transportation properties, the preferred stock would have to contain
redemption provisions—so that any retention of an
ownership interest would be of a temporary rather
than a permanent nature.

Petitioner, as above stated, was organized on
October 7, 1952, for the purpose of purchasing the
Transport Company's passenger transportation properties; and two days later, it entered into the contract
with the Transport Company to effectuate such purpose. The provisions of this purchase contract,
insofar as here material, are as follows:

SECTION 2. * * *

The base purchase price [of $10,000,000] to be paid by the Purchaser to the Seller at the closing shall be as follows:

(a) $4,000,000 in cash;

(b) $3,000,000 principal amount of the Purchaser's 5% Secured Promissory Notes, secured by a second mortgage covering the Purchaser's bondable transportation property, * * *; and

(c) 30,000 shares of the Purchaser's 5% Cumulative Preferred Stock, fully paid and non-assessable, having a par value of $100 per share, * * *

* * * * *

The Seller represents that it has no present intention of disposing of the 5% Secured Promissory Notes and the 5% Cumulative Preferred Stock of the Purchaser to be received by it under this Agreement, except to an associate company in the same holding company system, which will in turn acquire such securities with a view to holding them as an investment and not with a view to distribution.

SECTION 3. The purchaser agrees that prior to the closing it will issue and sell for cash at not less than the par or stated value thereof, Common Stock having a total par or stated value of at least Five-Hundred Thousand Dollars ($500,000).

* * * * *

Section 6. * * *

(b) The obligation of the Seller hereunder to convey the property to be sold hereunder is subject to the following conditions precedent:

1. That * * * counsel for the Purchaser shall have given an opinion to the Seller * * * that the 30,000 shares of 5% Cumulative Preferred Stock of the Purchaser to be delivered to the

Seller * * * are validly issued, fully paid and nonassessable.

*　　*　　*　　*　　*

SECTION 7. This agreement is made subject to obtaining all consents, authorizations and orders which shall be required by law to be obtained from any regulatory authority in order to carry out the terms of this Agreement, which each of the parties hereto agrees forthwith to apply for and to prosecute with due diligence; * * *.

Section 184.05(4) of the Wisconsin Statutes of 1951 (here applicable) provided in part as follows:

§ 184.05(4)—*Classes Proportionate.* The amount of securities of each class which any public service corporation may issue shall bear a reasonable proportion to each other and to the value of the property, * * *

Pursuant to the above-mentioned section 7 of the contract of purchase and the foregoing statutory provision, petitioner filed an application with the Wisconsin Public Service Commission for authority to issue the first mortgage bonds, the secured promissory notes, the preferred stock, and the common stock. Hearings were held; and the P.S.C., after finding that the issuance of the securities proposed to be issued complied with the relevant provisions of the Wisconsin Statutes and that the purchasers of said securities were afforded reasonable protection, certified on December 15, 1952, that petitioner was authorized to issue the securities, as requested.

In a statement accompanying the P.S.C.'s findings of fact and certificate, the Commission said:

[Effectuation of petitioner's proposed financing plan] will result in a capital structure and a ratio of each class of security to the total capitalization as follows:

	Amount	Ratio
First mortgage bonds	$4,000,000	38.1
Second mortgage notes	3,000,000	28.6
Total debt securities	7,000,000	66.7
Preferred stock	3,000,000	28.6
Common stock	500,000	4.7
Total capital structure	10,500,000	100.0

As indicated above, the proposed capital structure of the Suburban Company [the petitioner in the instant case] contains a disproportionate amount of securities senior to common stock. However, the secured promissory notes and preferred stock of the Suburban Company will not be in the hands of outside interests but will be owned initially by the Transport Company, which proposes to transfer the securities to the parent Electric Company. The application states that these securities will be held as an investment and not with a view to selling or distributing such securities.

In these circumstances it is concluded that the reasonable ratio provision of the statute does not bar the issuance of the securities as proposed. Further, in order to assure that an untimely distribution of the notes and preferred stock to the public is not made, the certificate herein will provide that the notes and preferred stock shall not be issued until the Suburban Company shall have obtained and filed with the Commission a written statement of the Electric Company agreeing not to sell or otherwise dispose of the notes or preferred stock (except through operation of the sinking fund) unless the authorization of the Commission to such sale or distribution shall have been obtained. * * *

During the pendency of petitioner's application before the P.S.C., the Transport Company's vice president, who also was an officer of the parent Power Company, transmitted to said Commission a forecast of petitioner's net income for the years 1953 through 1963. In such forecast which reflected the view of the seller, interest obligations on the first mortgage bonds and second mortgage notes were shown as deductions from gross income to arrive at net income; but dividends on the preferred stock were not so shown. Also, petitioner (the buyer) caused to be prepared and filed as an exhibit at said hearings, an estimate of its available cash for each of the years 1953 through 1959. In a supporting schedule attached to such estimate, the interest on the first mortgage bonds and second mortgage notes was deducted from operating income to arrive at net income before taxes; but the dividends on the preferred stock were deducted only after an amount representing net income after taxes had been computed. At such hearings and at all other times during the pendency of petitioner's application before the P.S.C., petitioner's representatives consistently referred to the preferred stock by that name; and at no time did they represent that such security evidenced a debt, or that it was anything other than preferred stock.

Shortly after the execution of the above-mentioned purchase contract, the Transport Company and the parent Power Company filed a joint "application-declaration" with the United States Securities and Exchange Commission, wherein they sought to have the S.E.C. approve the proposed sale of the Transport Company's public passenger transportation properties to petitioner. A hearing was held, at which an attorney representing petitioner entered an appearance and at which petitioner also produced a witness to testify regarding the proposed sale. Petitioner's witness did not represent the preferred stock to be evidence of a debt, or as anything other than preferred stock.

On December 24, 1952, the S.E.C. issued its findings and opinion and entered its order in the matter of the above-mentioned joint application-declaration, approving the proposed sale to petitioner. The Commission treated the proposed transaction as a plan for the simplification of the Power Company's holding company system; and it approved the sale, as being necessary to accomplish the divestiture required by the statute, and is being fair and equitable to the parent Power Company's security holders. In such findings and opinion, the Commission stated in part:

> We earlier noted that part of the consideration which Transport is to receive will consist of $3,000,000 of 5% Promissory Notes and $3,000,000 par value of 5% Cumulative Preferred Stock of New Transit Company [petitioner in the instant case]. As indicated previously, the securities to be issued by this company, and the terms thereof, are designed so as to bring about a gradual and relatively rapid retirement of the senior securities. Thus, the notes and preferred stock which Transport is to acquire are in no sense permanent investments such as would be precluded under the standards of Section 10 of the Act.

> *   *   *   *   *

> In appraising the effects of the proposed transactions, we have noted that the security structure of New Transit Company will include a rather large proportion of senior securities and, accordingly, the investment quality of the notes and preferred stock to be received by Transport will not, initially, be as good as might be desired. However, the record before us indicates that the New Transit Company should be able to make substantial reductions from year to year in the amount of senior securities outstanding. This, in turn, should result in a steady and material improvement in

the quality of the notes and preferred stock to be held by Transport.

In reaching our conclusion that the acquisition of the notes and preferred stock can be permitted under the standards of Section 10 of the Act, we point out that these securities are of such nature as would cause us to hesitate to approve their acquisition under ordinary circumstances. However, we are aware that such acquisition is desirable in the situation here present to enable Transport, as required by Section 11(b), to dispose of its passenger transportation business; but our approval of the acquisition of these securities is not intended as a finding that they can be retained indefinitely in the WEPCO [the parent Power Company] system under the standards of Section 11(b). Under the circumstances, we need not make any adverse findings * * *.

As above stated, petitioner's original capitalization at the time of its organization in October 1952, consisted of 10 shares of common capital stock, having a par value of $100 per share. On December 19, 1952, petitioner amended its articles of incorporation to increase its capitalization to $3,500,000 in anticipation of carrying out the proposed purchase of the public passenger transportation properties. Article III(a) of the amended articles of incorporation provided as follows:

(a) The capital stock of the corporation shall consist of 30,000 shares of Cumulative Preferred Stock of the par value of $100 each (hereinafter called "Preferred Stock") and 500,000 shares of Common Stock of the par value of $1.00 each (hereinafter called "Common Stock").

On December 30, 1952, the proposed transaction was consummated, and petitioner purchased the public passenger transportation properties of the Transport

Company. In connection therewith, petitioner issued 30,000 shares of $100 par value preferred stock to the Transport Company, as part of the agreed purchase price of $10,000,000. Such stock was designated on the certificates as "5% Cumulative Preferred Stock." The certificate for such preferred stock contained on the back thereof, the following material provisions:

(B) The holders of the preferred stock shall be entitled to receive, when and as declared by the board of directors, out of surplus or net profits, cumulative dividends in cash at the rate of 5% per annum and no more, payable quarter-yearly * * *. Such dividends on the preferred stock shall be cumulative from and after the 30th day of December, 1952.

(C) The corporation, at the option of the board of directors, may redeem the preferred stock at the time outstanding, in whole at any time or in part from time to time, upon notice duly given as hereinafter specified, by paying therefor in cash the par value thereof, together with a sum equal to 5% per annum on the par value thereof from the 30th day of December, 1952 to the date fixed for redemption, less the aggregate amount of all dividends theretofore paid thereon. * * *

(D) So long as any shares of the preferred stock remain outstanding, there shall be set aside [annually] as a sinking fund for the retirement of preferred stock, [beginning on a date 15 months after the first mortgage bonds and second mortgage notes had been retired] * * *'

(1) An amount in cash sufficient to redeem at the redemption price hereinabove provided 3,000 shares of preferred stock; and

(2) An amount in cash sufficient to redeem an aggregate par value of shares of preferred stock (to the nearest full share) equal to one-half of the net income of the corporation for

the above twelve months' period, determined
as hereinafter provided.

*   *   *   *   *

For the purposes of this paragraph (D) the
term "net income" shall mean [operating revenue, less operating expenses and dividends
on preferred stock, and plus or minus nonoperating income or nonoperating loss] * * *.

(E) In case of liquidation, dissolution or
winding up of the corporation * * *, the holders of preferred stock shall be entitled to receive the par value thereof in the distribution
of corporation assets, other than profits, before
any such assets shall be paid or distributed to
holders of common stock, and to receive out
of the earned surplus or net profits, or other
legal sources then permitted for the payment
of such dividends all accumulated and unpaid
dividends before any payment is made or distributed out of such surplus, net profits or
other legal sources to the holders of common
stock.

(F) [In substance, petitioner was forbidden
to merge, consolidate, or sell or lease substantially all its assets without the consent of the
holders of two-thirds of the outstanding preferred stock.]

(G) [In substance and so far as here
material, so long as any of the preferred stock
was outstanding, petitioner was limited in the
amount of indebtedness which it could incur,
to: (1) Short-term borrowings of $500,000;
(2) the $4,000,000 of first mortgage bonds; (3)
the $3,000,000 of secured promissory notes; and
(4) long-term borrowings of $1,500,000, until
$2,000,000 of the first mortgage bonds had been
retired, and $2,500,000 of such borrowings
thereafter.]

(H) Except as otherwise provided by statute or by subdivisions (F), (G) and (I)
hereof, voting rights for all purposes shall be

23

vested exclusively in the holders of the common stock, * * *.

(I) [In substance and so far as here material, the holders of the preferred stock were accorded the "special right" of electing the smallest number of directors required to constitute a majority of petitioner's board of directors: (1) if and when dividends on the preferred stock were in default for eight quarters; or (2) if the petitioner corporation should have defaulted in setting aside the amounts for the sinking fund, as required in paragraph (D). The foregoing "special right" of the holders of the preferred stock was to be divested, and the term of the directors elected thereunder terminated, as soon as the default was cured.]

(J) [In substance and so far as here material, petitioner was forbidden, so long as any of the preferred stock was outstanding, to declare and pay cash dividends on its common stock, unless all dividends due at that time on the preferred stock had been paid, and unless there had been set aside the amounts required for the sinking fund.]

(K) [In substance, the holders of the preferred stock were not entitled to pre-emptive rights, with respect to any new or additional securities which petitioner might issue.]

Petitioner's attorneys advised the Transport Company in a letter dated December 30, 1952, in part as follows:

6. The 30,000 shares of Preferred Stock, a temporary certificate for which has been delivered to you today, are validly issued, fully paid and non-assessable. * * *

The preferred stock was entered on petitioner's books of account, in account number 2302, entitled "Preferred Capital Stock." In published annual reports to its stockholders, petitioner described such stock as 5 percent cumulative preferred stock.

The management of the Transport Company believed that it was getting preferred stock having redemptive provisions.

For each of the years 1953 and 1954, petitioner paid to the holders of its preferred stock $150,000 as "dividends" on the same.

The Transport Company, in the course of the negotiations with the organizers of petitioner, had considered that payments to be received in respect of such preferred stock would be dividends, and that it would be entitled on its Federal income tax returns, to an 85 percent dividends received credit or deduction, with respect to the same. On its return for the years 1953 and 1954, dividends received credits or deductions were claimed.

Petitioner, on its Federal income tax returns for each of the years 1953 and 1954, deducted as "interest" the amount of its payments with respect to the preferred stock. But respondent, in his statutory notices of deficiency, disallowed said claimed deductions.

Petitioner, in computing on its 1953 return its excess profits credit based on invested capital, included the $3,000,000 of preferred stock in its borrowed capital (as distinguished from equity invested capital); and only 75 percent of such amount was taken into account in computing its excess profits credit. This action did not effect any change in the amount of petitioner's excess profits tax liability.

Opinion (Issue I)

When the parties came to selecting the type of security which was to supplement the first mortgage bonds and the second mortgage notes and the common stock, they found themselves impaled on the horns of a dilemma. Their task was to find a type of security which would sufficiently resemble debt to satisfy the S.E.C. that the Transport Company had divested itself of its passenger transportation properties; and, on the other hand, to satisfy the P.S.C. that the security represented an equity investment, in order to obtain the latter's approval of the issues of such security. Presumably, petitioner wanted interest deductions for the periodic payments which it was to make, and has made, with respect to this security; while, on the other hand, the Transport Company wanted the payments which it was to receive, to qualify as dividend payments, so that it might be entitled to dividends received credits or deductions with respect thereto. The result, as might well have been expected, was the creation of a hybrid, which is neither a pure debt security nor a pure equity security, but which has some of the characteristics of each. Our task, in deciding the present issue (whether, despite the label of "dividends," the payments were in substance "interest on indebtedness"), is to put this security in either a debt category or an equity category.

The present issue is by no means one of first impression. Some of the criteria which have been developed by the courts to aid in the difficult task of pigeonholing these hybrids, are: What name did the parties give to the instrument? Does the instrument have a definite maturity date? What is the source from which the "dividends" or "interest," as well as the redemption payments, will be paid? Does a holder of such security have a right to participate in the management of the issuing corporation? What rights does a holder have in the event of default in payment by the issuer? Does a holder have preference on liquidation over general creditors? What was the original intention of the issuer and the recipient of the security, as evidenced by all the surrounding facts and circumstances? Would classification of the security as an evidence of debt, produce a disproportionate amount of debt in relation to equity capital? See *Kingsmill Corporation*, 28 T.C. 3330; Mertens, Law of Federal Income Taxation, Vol. 4, §§ 26.10, 26.10a and 26.10c.

Applying the foregoing criteria to the facts of the instant case, we have concluded that the security here involved represents an equity investment. Therefore, the payments made by petitioner with respect to the same are "dividends," which are not deductible for Federal tax purposes.

The characteristics of the instrument, which evidences the security involved, are predominantly those of an equity security. The instrument is plainly denominated, on its face, as preferred stock. It recites that the holder may become entitled to receive "cumulative dividends," but only when declared by petitioner's board of directors; and the source of such payments, so the instrument provides, shall be "surplus or net profits." The holder has preference on liquidation, dissolution, or a winding up of the petitioner, over the common stockholders, but not over general creditors. On failure of petitioner to pay dividends for eight consecutive quarters, or on its failure to set aside amounts for the sinking fund, the holder's sole remedy is to take over direction of the corporation (by electing a sufficient number of directors to constitute a majority of the board of directors) until the default is cured. It is true that the provisions for a sinking fund do point to an intention on petitioner's part to repay the par value of the preferred stock, without regard to the existence of profits; but it should be observed that the obligation to set aside any amount for the sinking fund arises only after the first mortgage bonds and the second mortgage notes are paid off. Thus, there is neither a fixed obligation to pay the par value of the preferred stock, nor a fixed and definite maturity date. And, even if it were possible to construe the provisions of the preferred stock certificate as providing a fixed maturity date, that would not be conclusive as to the existence of a debtor-creditor relationship. *Lee Telephone Co. v. Commissioner* (C.A. 4), 260 F. 2d 114, affirming T.C. Memo. 1957-230; *Commissioner v. Meridian & Thirteenth R. Co.* (C.A. 7), 132 F. 2d 182. After considering all the foregoing, we think that the security itself points more toward an equity than toward a debt.

Furthermore, the circumstances leading up to and surrounding the creation and issuance of the security involved, impel us to the same conclusion—that the security represents an equity investment. In the initial negotiations, the principal negotiator on behalf of the Transport Company made it clear to the persons who were to organize the petitioner, that the security involved would have to qualify as an equity security, if the requisite approval by the P.S.C. was to be had; and said persons agreed. This same chief negotiator testified in the instant case, that his company had always intended to receive preferred stock. And said company, consistent with its belief that it did get preferred stock, has always regarded the payments which it received, to be dividends; and it has, for Federal tax purposes, uniformly availed itself of the dividends received credit or deduction, with respect thereto.

Also, at the hearings before the P.S.C. and the S.E.C., the security was represented to be preferred stock, and nothing else. And documentary evidence submitted to each of these public bodies, both by petitioner and by the Transport Company, indicated that the payments with respect to the security were to be dividends. Thereafter, petitioner amended its articles of incorporation, and therein provided that the security here in dispute was to be preferred stock. And its counsel, as required by the terms of the purchase contract, then advised the Transport Company that it was being issued preferred stock.

Petitioner has at all times carried the security on its books, in an account entitled "Preferred Capital Stock." It also has so described the security in reports to its shareholders. Although petitioner in the excess profits schedule of its 1953 return, characterized the security as borrowed rather than invested capital, this can not be given too much weight because, even in the absence of such characterization, petitioner would have had no excess profits tax liability for that year.

Moreover, the P.S.C., which approved the issuance of the securities, made findings of fact and issued a certificate of approval, in which (as shown in our Findings of Fact) it listed the first mortgage bonds and the second mortgage notes as debt securities, but did not so list the preferred stock. Also, it recited therein that the petitioner's application had represented that the preferred stock "will be held as an investment"; and stated that its certificate of approval would not be issued, until the parent Power Company had given assurance that the preferred stock would not be disposed of without prior approval of the Commission.

Also as regards the S.E.C., a reading of its findings and opinion convince us that said Commission recognized that, despite the divestiture requirement of the

Federal statute, the Transport Company retained through the preferred stock, an investment in petitioner. It is apparent that this Commission would rather have had a more complete severance on the part of the Transport Company; but it appears to have recognized that the transaction which it approved, was as complete a divestiture as could be expected in the circumstances.

Finally, it should be observed that, if the preferred stock were classed as evidence of a debt, petitioner would have a capital structure made up of 95.3 percent debt and only 4.7 percent equity, or a ratio of debt to equity of 20 to 1. On the other hand, if the preferred stock is classed as equity capital, the ratio of debt to equity is the much more realistic one of 2 to 1. Considering the magnitude of the mass public transportation business in the City of Milwaukee, it seems unrealistic to expect that petitioner could acquire and operate such a business with only $500,000 of equity capital.

For all of the foregoing reasons, we sustain the respondent's determination as to this issue. Compare *Lee Telephone Co.* v. *Commissioner, supra; Commissioner* v. *Meridian & Thirteenth R. Co., supra; Kingsmill Corporation, supra.*

Such action makes it unnecessary for us to consider the incidental questions, relating to the deductibility of the expense of issuing the security involved, and relating to the claimed net operating loss carryover deduction which is based on the deductibility both of said expense and of the payments made on such security. Petitioner appears to have recognized in its pleadings (and we agree) that the deductibility of these incidental items is dependent upon a determination that the preferred stock represents an indebtedness. And having held that such stock represents an equity investment rather than an indebtedness, we approve the respondent's disallowance of the deductions for said items.

II. Issue re Accruability of Estimated Liability for Property Damages and Personal Injuries

FINDINGS OF FACT

During each of the taxable years 1953 and 1954, petitioner operated approximately 1,000 vehicles, including street cars, trolley buses, and gasoline and diesel buses. It carried approximately 281 million passengers in 1953, and 250 million passengers in 1954; and in each of these years, petitioner's passenger vehicles were operated in excess of 33 million miles. In 1953, petitioner's operating vehicles were involved in 5,903 accidents; and in 1954 the number of accidents was 5,041.

During each of the taxable years, petitioner carried what is called "excess public liability insurance," to cover the operation of its motor buses and other vehicles, under policies which insured against liability of petitioner for property damages and personal injuries occasioned by any one accident, to the extent that such liability should exceed $100,000 but be less than $1,000,000. This was petitioner's only liability insurance coverage. As to liability for property damages and personal injuries in amounts less than $100,000, petitioner sought from the Motor Vehicle Department of the State of Wisconsin, and was granted, the right to act as a self-insurer.

Petitioner maintained a staff of attorneys and claim adjusters to investigate accidents occurring in the course of the operation of its vehicles, to effect settlements, and to defend petitioner in suits brought by parties injured or damaged in such accidents. As a result of investigations made by the attorneys and claim adjusters, settlement of the great majority of the accident claims made against petitioner was affected during the same year that the accident occurred.

As of December 31, 1953, there were 414 claims unsettled. And as of December 31, 1954, there were 447 unsettled claims growing out of accidents occurring in such year. Also, some of the claims unsettled as at December 31, 1953, remained unsettled at the end of the year 1954.

At the end of each of the years 1953 and 1954, petitioner's board of directors appointed from their number, a committee of three (two of whom were attorneys) to examine the information gathered by petitioner's attorneys and claim adjusters relating to each of the unsettled claims, and to determine whether in such committee's opinion petitioner was liable, and to what extent. The committee members were assisted in their work for both taxable years, by the petitioner's general claim agent; and in the first of such years they were assisted also by a certified public accountant from the firm which audited petitioner's books of account.

In January 1954, the committee made a report to the board of directors of its findings with respect to the unsettled claims pending as of December 31, 1953. The committee estimated that petitioner's liability with respect to the 414 pending claims for that year was $254,659; and the committee authorized the general claim agent to dispose of these several claims at the amounts at which they had been appraised. Petitioner's board of directors ratified and confirmed its committee's action. Also, the committee made a similar report in January 1955, relating to the unsettled claims arising out of 1954 accidents; estimated petitioner's liability with respect to the 447 pending claims for said year to be $161,136.50; and authorized the general claim agent to dispose of such pending claims at the amounts at which they had been appraised. The committee's action with respect to unsettled claims of the year 1954 was likewise ratified and confirmed by the board of directors.

Petitioner did not at any time notify, or otherwise admit to, any of the claimants that it considered itself liable; nor did it make an offer to any claimant to settle his claim at the amount at which such claim had been appraised. It always sought to settle claims at the lowest possible figure.

As of December 31, 1953, petitioner set up on its books of account, as a book liability for unsettled claims, the above-mentioned amount of $254,659; and it also debited a related expense account for injuries and damages, in the same amount. On its Federal income tax return for the year 1953, petitioner claimed a deduction for said amount of $254,659.

As regards the taxable year 1954, petitioner, as of December 31, 1954, increased its aforesaid liability account by the amount of $142,022.87, and debited its related expense account for the same amount. On its 1954 income tax return, it claimed a deduction for said amount of $142,022.87, which was computed as follows:

Appraised liability on unsettled claims, 1954 accidents		$161,136.50
Deduct: Appraised liability of 1953 claims settled in 1954	$94,984.00	
Less: Amounts at which 1953 claims were actually settled	75,870.87	19,113.63
Net amount expensed and added to liability account		142,022.87

The respondent, in his statutory notices of deficiency, disallowed the entire amount of $254,659, which was claimed as a deduction on petitioner's 1953 return; and he also disallowed $61,472.79 of the $142,022.87 which was claimed as a deduction on petitioner's 1954 return.[1] The respondent allowed as a deduction in each taxable year, the amount of the claims for injuries and damages which actually were settled by the petitioner in each such year.

The claimants in 22 of the 414 unsettled claims for the year 1953 began suit against petitioner on or before December 31 of said year; and during 1954, claimants in 16 of the 447 claims unsettled as of December 31 of said year began suit against petitioner. Of the 22 claims for the year 1953 which were in litigation at the end of said year, 3 of the same were still in litigation at August 31, 1958; and of the 16 claims on which litigation had been begun during the year 1954 (and which were still in litigation at the end of said year), 9 of the same were still in litigation on August 31, 1958.

With respect to each of the claims which was in litigation at the end of each of the years 1953 and 1954, petitioner denied liability in its pleadings for such cases.

In addition to the claims in litigation above mentioned, other unsettled claims arising out of accidents which had occurred in each of the taxable years were put into litigation after the close of each such year. Suit was thus begun on 31 of the claims pending at December 31, 1953, and on 32 of the claims pending at December 31, 1954. All claims on which litigation

---

[1] The record does not contain the computation which the respondent used to arrive at the amount disallowed for 1954. From a computation suggested by the petitioner in its briefs, it appears that the disallowance represents the difference between the claimed deduction, and the amount of the 1953 claims settled in 1954.

was begun after the close of the taxable years were settled on or before August 31, 1958.

Many potential claims with respect to which the committee of petitioner's board of directors determined that petitioner was liable and with respect to which estimates of the amounts of liability were made, never progressed beyond the point of reports made to petitioner by its employees; for the injured parties neither presented claims to petitioner nor filed suit against it. There were 138 and 144 of such situations, involving estimated liabilities of $34,470 and $26,521, for the taxable years 1953 and 1954, respectively. The statute of limitations had run against any suit for the same by the time of the trial of the present case; and petitioner will not have to make any payment with respect thereto.

All claims pending at the end of each taxable year (other than those litigated and those not pressed by the injured parties) were settled after the close of such years, without the necessity for resort to litigation.

The committee of petitioner's board of directors determined the petitioner had no liability in respect of 15 of the unsettled claims pending at December 31, 1953, and in respect of 49 of the unsettled claims pending at December 31, 1954. But nevertheless, petitioner ultimately made settlements, whereunder it paid sums of money to the claimants in 14 of such 1953 claims and in 43 of such 1954 claims.

As regards claims wherein the committee had estimated that petitioner was liable and settlements were made (either with or without litigation), the settlement amounts were equal to the estimates in only 31 out of 261 of such 1953 claims, and in only 22 out of 254 of such claims. Settlements were at variance

with estimates by more than 100 percent in 97 of said
1953 claims and in 102 of said 1954 claims.

As regards claims which were still unsettled at
the time of the trial herein, only those listed in the
following table were then regarded by the petitioner
to be still open; and the amounts shown opposite each
of such claims represent petitioner's original estimates, and its current estimates at the time of the
trial herein, of its liability with respect to the same:

Claim number	Year 1953	
	Original estimate	Current estimate
4	$150	$400
23	100	1,500
71	100	1,500
90	1,700	800
100	500	3,500
108	750	3,500
212	400	2,500
263	1,500	800
	5,200	14,560

Claim number	Year 1954	
	Original estimate	Current estimate
416	$300	$1,500
419	3,500	2,000
442	2,000	7,000
467	750	2,000
474	350	3,000
505	300	3,500
513	1,000	10,000
523	1,500	15,000
554	200	150
558	750	1,500
589	500	2,500
639	1,000	2,500
670	600	765
	12,750	51,415

The differences between the above current estimates
and the above original estimates were, in all instances,
due to circumstances which could not have been fore-
seen at the time when the original estimates were
made.

The following table shows a comparison of petitioner's estimates of its total liability for unsettled claims at the end of each of the taxable years, with the total amounts actually paid out in settlements thereof:

Year	Number of claims	Petitioner's estimated liability	Payments actually made in settlement of same through Aug. 31, 1958
1953	414	*$254,659.00	$178,230.24
1954	447	**161,136.50	159,851.84

*Includes $34,470, representing 138 unpressed claims.
**Includes $26,521, representing 144 unpressed claims.

Opinion (Issue I)

The question here presented is whether petitioner, an accrual basis taxpayer, may deduct for each of the years 1953 and 1954, certain amounts accrued by it on its books of account as of December 31 of each year. Such amounts represented its estimate of the probable amounts which it would have to pay in settlement for personal injuries and property damages, arising out of accidents in which its employees and equipment were involved.

As hereinbefore shown in our Findings of Fact, equipment operated by petitioner's employees was involved in more than 5,000 accidents in each of the taxable years; and the bulk of the claims for damages arising out of these accidents in a particular year were settled during the course of such year. However, at the end of each taxable year, there were approximately 400 claims still pending, some of which were in litigation, and as to all of which petitioner denied liability. A committee, appointed by petitioner's board of directors and assisted by its general claim agent and an accountant, currently examined the available data with respect to such unsettled claims; and they then determined whether in their opinion petitioner was liable therefor, and to what extent. The general claim agent was authorized by the committee to settle each of the pending claims for the amount at which it was appraised; and the committee's action was thereafter ratified and approved by the petitioner's board of directors. For the taxable year 1953, petitioner set up on its books as an accrued liability and as a related accrued expense, the total amount estimated by the committee to be petitioner's liability for unsettled claims. And for 1954, it similarly set up on its books amounts which (as shown in our Findings of Fact) were somewhat less than the committee's estimates. We must here decided whether the amount so accrued as an expense for each year constitutes an allowable deduction for Federal income tax purposes.

It is a well settled principle of law, that two conditions must be fulfilled before an expense becomes accruable and deductible for Federal income tax purposes: (1) During the taxable year all events must have occurred which establish in the taxpayer a definite liability to pay such expense; and (2) the amount of such liability must be determinable within the taxable year, with reasonable certainty. *Dixie Pine Products Co.* v. *Commissioner,* 320 U.S. 516; *Anderson* v. *United States,* 269 U.S. 422; *Uncasville Mfg. Co.* v. *Commissioner,* 55 F. 2d 893; *Ralph L. Patsch,* 19 T.C. 195, aff'd. (C.A. 3) 208 F. 2d 532. Where the taxpayer is contesting his liability, no accrual may be made for tax purposes until the contest ends. *Dixie Pine Products Co.* v. *Commissioner, supra; Security Flour Mills Co.* v. *Commissioner,* 321 U.S. 281; *Denver & Rio Grande Western Railroad Co.,* 32 T.C. 43.

Applying the foregoing legal standards to the facts of the instant case, it becomes apparent from the following that the amounts accrued by petitioner on its books as expenses for estimated liabilities, do not meet either of the above-mentioned conditions precedent to accrual.

First, the existence of petitioner's liability respecting the unsettled claims of each year did not become definitely fixed during such year. Several of the claims were acutally in litigation at the end of each year; and as to these, petitioner's pleadings in the lawsuits denied any liability. As to all remaining claims (many of which were put in litigation after the close of the taxable years in which they arose), petitioner did not during such years admit its liability to any claimant. And, though petitioner's general claim agent was vested with authority to settle the pending claims at the amounts estimated by its board's committee, said agent testified that petitioner did not make any offer to settle the claims at the appraised figures, but contrariwise sought to settle each claim at the lowest possible figure. We conclude that petitioner's liability as to each unsettled claim was contested; and that there was not within either of the taxable years, any definitely fixed liability to pay any unsettled claim pending as of the end of such year.

Secondly, the amount of petitioner's liability in respect of unsettled claims of each year was not ascertainable within such year, with reasonable certainty. Only 31 of the 261 claims for 1953, with respect to which estimates of liability had been made and with respect to which settlements were ultimately effected, were settled by petitioner for amounts equal to the estimates of liability; and for the year 1954, only 22 of the 254 such claims were ultimately settled for amounts which tallied with the estimates. As regards those claims for which petitioner estimated that it was liable, the settlements were at variance with the estimates by more than 100 percent, in 97 of the claims for 1953 and in 102 of the claims for 1954. Many other settlements in each year varied more than 50 percent from the estimates of liability. In respect of numerous unsettled claims of each year, petitioner estimated that it had no liability; but in the overwhelming majority of these cases, it did make monetary settlements with the claimants. Also, many of the so-called claims were only potential claims which never were pressed by the injured parties, and as to which petitioner has not made and will not make any payment. Furthermore, as to the unsettled claims which petitioner considered to be still open at the time of the trial herein, the table in our Findings of Fact shows that petitioner's current estimates of its liability are, in most instances, widely at variance with its original estimates; and petitioner's general claim agent testified that this was due to unforeseeable conditions arising after the original estimates had been made. In the light of all the foregoing, it is manifest that petitioner could not estimate the bulk of its potential liabilities with even approximate, not to say reasonable, certainty.

In substance what petitioner is here attempting to do, is to take deductions for amounts used to create, and to supplement, a reserve for contingent liabilities in respect of unsettled and potential claims for property damage and personal injury. But, as we said in deciding the seventh issue in the recent case of *Denver & Rio Grande Western Railroad Co., supra:*

> [A] reserve for contingent liabilities of this kind [contingent liabilities almost identical with those here involved] has never been allowed under any of the Revenue Acts or Internal Revenue Codes. *Lucas v. American Code Co.,* 280 U.S. 445; *Richmond Light &*

Railroad Co., supra [4 B.T.A. 91]; *Ralph L. Patsch,* 19 T.C. 189, affd. 208 F. 2d 532.

Also, even in the very early case of *William J. Ostheimer,* 1 B.T.A. 18, we said:

> While it might have been sound business practice on the part of the taxpayer to set up a reserve out of his income to meet a *future* liability, such a reserve is not deductible in determining net income.

Petitioner has, however, vigorously pressed upon us the argument that, while considered individually the unsettled claims were contested and unsusceptible of accurate determination; yet, if the unsettled claims of each year are viewed in the aggregate, it can be taken as certain that petitioner will have some liability and that estimates of its total net liability with respect to the aggregate of each year's unsettled claims can be determined. It cites in this connection, two cases: *Ocean Accident & Guarantee Corporation, Ltd.* v. *Commissioner,* (C.A. 2) 47 F. 2d 582, reversing 13 B.T.A. 1057 and 16 B.T.A. 1313; and *Pacific Employers Insurance Co.,* 33 B.T.A. 501. In each of these cases the taxpayer was an insurance company, and it was allowed to deduct accrued estimates of its unpaid liabilities. But, the answers to petitioner's argument, and also the distinction between the cited cases and the instant case, are provided by the following quotation from the Supreme Court's opinion in *Brown* v. *Helvering,* 291 U.S. 193, wherein the court said:

> The liability of **Edward Brown & Sons** [a general agent for insurance companies] arising from expected future cancellations was not deductible from gross income because it was not fixed and absolute. In respect to no particular policy written within the year could it be known that it would be canceled in a future

year. Nor could it be known that a definite percentage of all the policies will be canceled in the future years. Experience taught that there is a strong probability that many of the policies written during the taxable year will be so canceled. But experience taught also that we are not dealing here with certainties. This is shown by the variations in the percentages in the several five-year periods of the aggregate of refunds to the aggregate of over-riding commissions.

Brown argues that, since insurance companies are allowed to deduct reserves for unearned premiums which may have to be refunded, he should be allowed to make the deductions claimed as being similar in character. The simple answer is that the general agent is not an insurance company; and that the deductions allowed for additions to the reserves of insurance companies are technical in character and are specifically provided for in the Revenue Acts. These technical reserves are required to be made by the insurance laws of the several states. * * *

The respondent apparently has allowed to petitioner those portions of its claimed deductions for the liabilities here involved which represent the amounts of the settlements actually made in each of the taxable years, in respect of such liabilities. We think that the allowance of only such amounts produces a more clear reflection of income than would the allowance of the exceedingly rough estimates made by petitioner of its liabilities for potential and unsettled claims. On the basis of the authorities above cited, we hold that the amounts allowed by respondent are the maximum amounts to which petitioner is entitled; and we approve the respondent's determinations as to the present issue.

Decisions will be entered for the respondent.

September Term and Session, 1960

No. 13025

Milwaukee & Suburban Transport Corporation,
Petitioner

v.

Commissioner of Internal Revenue, Respondent

PETITION FOR REVIEW OF DECISION OF THE TAX COURT OF
THE UNITED STATES

October 24, 1960

Before Duffy and Knoch, *Circuit Judges*, and
Grubb, *District Judge*.

Grubb, *District Judge*. This is a petition for review
of a decision by the tax court disallowing certain deductions by the petitioner in the years 1953 and 1954.
There are two issues, one involving the preferred
stock of the petitioner and the other involving its
accounting method.

PREFERRED STOCK ISSUE

Petitioner is a corporation organized on October 7,
1952, under the laws of the State of Wisconsin. It
filed its returns for the taxable years 1953 and 1954
with the Director of Internal Revenue for the District of Wisconsin. It kept its books of account and
filed its Federal income tax returns in accordance

with an accrual method of accounting and on the basis of calendar years.

In the year 1952 and for several years prior thereto, the public passenger transportation system in the City of Milwaukee and its environs was owned and operated by the Milwaukee Electric Railway and Transport Company (hereinafter called the "Transport Company") which was a wholly owned subsidiary of the Wisconsin Electric Power Company (hereinafter called the "Power Company"). Both the parent and the subsidiary were Wisconsin corporations, and the parent also was a registered public utility holding company subject to the provisions of the Federal Public Utility Holding Company Act of 1935 (Title 15 U.S.C., Section 79).

During the 1940's the management of the Power Company and of the Transport Company came to realize that by reason of the provisions of the Public Utility Holding Company Act of 1935, it would be necessary to remove the public passenger transportation properties owned by the subsidiary Transport Company from the holding company system of the parent Power Company.

On December 30, 1952, the petitioner purchased the transportation facilities of the Transport Company. The purchase price of $10,000,000 was payable in the following manner: $4,000,000 in cash to be raised by the sale of bonds to outside parties which would be secured by a first mortgage on the assets; $3,000,000 of the petitioner's promissory notes to be issued to the Transport Company and which were secured by a second mortgage; and $3,000,000 in preferred stock to be issued to the Transport Company. In addition, the organizers of the petitioner were to invest a total of $500,000 in common stock of the petitioner in order to supply working capital.

The tax court found as fact that:

"* * * it was the belief of the parties that, if the issuance of the securities by the purchasing corporation was to receive the required approval of the Public Service Commission of Wisconsin (hereinafter called the P.S.C.), the ratio of corporate debt to equity capital could not be too high. Also it was believed that, if the sale was to receive the required approval of the United States Securities and Exchange Commission (hereinafter called the S.E.C.), as a divestiture by the Power Company of the public passenger transportation properties, the preferred stock would have to contain redemption provisions—so that any retention of an ownership interest would be of a temporary rather than a permanent nature."

The material provisions of the purchase contract follow:

"SECTION 2. * * *

"The base purchase price [of $10,000,000] to be paid by the Purchaser to the Seller at the closing shall be as follows:

"(a) $4,000,000 in cash;

"(b) $3,000,000 principal amount of the Purchaser's 5% Secured Promissory Notes, secured by a second mortgage covering the Purchaser's bondable transportation property, * * *; and

"(c) 30,000 shares of the Purchaser's 5% Cumulative Preferred Stock, fully paid and nonassessable, having a par value of $100 per share, * * *.

* * * * *

"The Seller represents that it has no present intention of disposing of the 5% Secured Promissory Notes and the 5% Cumulative Preferred Stock of the Purchaser to be received by it under this Agreement, except to an associate company in the same holding company system, which will in turn acquire such securities with a view to holding them as an investment and not with a view to distribution.

"SECTION 3. The purchaser agrees that prior to the closing it will issue and sell for cash at not less than the par or stated value thereof, Common Stock having a total par or stated value of at least Five-Hundred Thousand Dollars ($500,000).

* * * * *

"SECTION 6. * * *

"(b) The obligation of the Seller hereunder to convey the property to be sold hereunder is subject to the following conditions precedent:

"1. That * * * counsel for the Purchaser shall have given an opinion to the Seller * * * that the 30,000 shares of 5% Cumulative Preferred Stock of the Purchaser to be delivered to the Seller * * * are validly issued, fully paid and non-assessable.

* * * * *

"Section 7. This agreement is made subject to obtaining all consents, authorizations and orders which shall be required by law to be obtained from any regulatory authority in order to carry out the terms of this Agreement, which each of the parties hereto agrees forthwith to apply for and to prosecute with due diligence; * * *."

Article III(a) of the petitioner's amended articles of incorporation provides as follows:

"(a) The capital stock of the corporation shall consist of 30,000 shares of Cumulative Preferred Stock of the par value of $100 each (hereinafter called 'Preferred Stock') and 500,000 shares of Common Stock of the par value of $1.00 each (hereinafter called 'Common Stock')."

The preferred stock certificate contained the following provisions:

"(B) The holders of the preferred stock shall be entitled to receive, when and as declared by the board of directors, out of surplus or net profits, cumulative dividends in cash at the rate of 5% per annum and no more, payable quarter-yearly * * *. Such dividends on the preferred stock shall be cumulative from and after the 30th day of December, 1952.

"(C) The corporation, at the option of the board of directors, may redeem the preferred stock at the time outstanding, in whole at any time or in part from time to time, upon notice duly given as hereinafter specified, by paying therefor in cash the par value thereof, together with a sum equal to 5% per annum on the par value thereof from the 30th day of December, 1952 to the date fixed for redemption, less the aggregate amount of all dividends theretofore paid thereon. * * *

"(D) So long as any shares of the preferred stock remain outstanding, there shall be set aside [annually] as a sinking fund for the retirement of preferred stock, [beginning on a date 15 months after the first mortgage bonds and second mortgage notes had been retired] * * *,

"(1) An amount in cash sufficient to redeem at the redemption price hereinabove provided 3,000 shares of preferred stock; and

"(2) An amount in cash sufficient to redeem an aggregate par value of shares of preferred stock (to the nearest full share) equal to one-half of the net income of the corporation for the above twelve months' period, determined as hereinafter provided.

*   *   *   *   *

"For the purposes of this paragraph (D) the term 'net income' shall mean [operating revenue, less operating expenses and dividends on preferred stock, and plus or minus nonoperating income or nonoperating loss] * * *."

Petitioner's attorney advised the Transport Company in a letter dated December 30, 1952, as follows:

"6. The 30,000 shares of Preferred Stock, a temporary certificate for which has been delivered to you today, are validly issued, fully paid and non-assessable. * * *"

The preferred stock was entered on petitioner's books in an account entitled "Preferred Stock." In its annual reports the stock was referred to as preferred stock.

Applications were filed with the Public Service Commission and the Securities Exchange Commission for authority to consummate the transaction, and after various hearings were held, authorization was ultimately obtained. In all proceedings before both of these bodies. the stock in question was always referred to and represented to be preferred stock.

Petitioner, on its tax returns for 1953 and 1954, deducted as "interest" the amount of its payments with respect to the preferred stock, but these deductions were disallowed by the respondent.

The question involved in this issue is whether the security denominated "preferred stock" is a debt or an equity investment. Although there are factors present which favor the taxpayer, the court is of the opinion that there is sufficient support in the record for the tax court's conclusion that the petitioner's payments to preferred stockholders in the years 1953 and 1954 were actually, as well as in form, dividends and not interest and thus nondeductible.

In *Commissioner of Internal Revenue* v. *Meridian & Thirteenth Realty Co.*, 132 F. 2d 182 (7th Cir. 1942), this court made the following statement in a case very similar to the instant one at page 186:

"It is often said that the essential difference between a creditor and a stockholder is that the

latter intends to make an investment and take
the risks of the venture, while the former seeks
a definite obligation, payable in any event.
* * *"

The securities involved in the present case undoubtedly have certain characteristics which would in-
dicate that the investment was not subject to the risks
of the venture. For instance, there appears to be a
definite maturity date for the stock had to be redeemed by March 1, 1972, at the latest, although an
earlier retirement dependent upon the earnings of the
corporation was possible. In addition, on the basis
of the contract as influenced by Wisconsin corporation law, the redemption price apparently could be
paid out of capital or capital surplus and was not dependent on earnings. These factors are persuasive
but are not conclusive of the question. *John Kelley
Co. v. Commissioner of Internal Revenue*, 326 U.S.
521 (1946); *Commissioner of Internal Revenue v.
Meridian & Thirteenth Realty Co., supra;* and *Lee
Telephone Co. v. Commissioner of Internal Revenue*,
260 F. 2d 114 (4th Cir. 1958).

As intimated earlier, there are other elements which
tend to water down the significance of the above-
mentioned factors. The maturity date, for example,
is contingent to a certain degree for the preferred
stock sinking fund does not commence until after
$7,000,000 of bonds and notes are retired. The prob-
abilities are that that these securities will be paid off
on schedule, but this is not certain, and, consequently,
the maturity date could theoretically be pushed back
well beyond the 1972 date.

In addition, the practical effect of such a situation
beyond casting a shadow on the definiteness of the
maturity date is to subordinate the preferred stock
to the debt represented by the bonds and notes. Since,

as will be shown later, the preferred stock is also subordinated to general creditors, it is clear that it is very much subject to the risks of the venture.

Under pertinent Wisconsin statutes [2] it appears that the preferred stock could be redeemed out of funds other than earnings. The redemption is restricted as the redemption can only be made if the corporation would not be rendered insolvent. Thus, it is clear that the preferred stock is in fact subordinated to general creditors.

Another characteristic of the preferred stock which tends to support the conclusion of the tax court is the fact that the charter restricts *current* dividends to earnings. Thus, although deferred cumulative dividends could be paid out of capital surplus at redemp-

---

[2] 1951 Wisconsin Statutes—"180.38 *dividends*. * * * (3) The board of directors of a corporation may also, from time to time, distribute to the holders of its outstanding shares having a cumulative preferential right to receive dividends, in discharge of their cumulative dividend rights, dividends payable in cash out of the capital surplus of the corporation, if at the time the corporation has no earned surplus and is not insolvent and would not thereby be rendered insolvent. Each such distribution, when made, shall be identified as a payment of cumulative dividends out of capital surplus."

1951 Wisconsin Statutes—"180.05 *Power of corporation to acquire and dispose of its own shares.* (1) A corporation shall have power to purchase, take, receive, redeem in accordance with their terms, or otherwise acquire, hold, own, pledge, transfer, or otherwise dispose of its own shares; provided that no such acquisition, directly or indirectly, of its own shares for a consideration other than its own shares of equal or subordinate rank shall be made unless all of the following conditions are met:

"(a) At the time of such acquisition the corporation is not and would not thereby be rendered insolvent: * * *"

See also 1953 Wisconsin Statutes, Sections 180.38(3) and 180.385(1)(a).

tion, current dividends are restricted to earnings. Also, there are various provisions on the preferred stock certificate, such as that conferring the right to participate in management upon default, which are typical to any preferred stock.

In addition to the characteristics of the security, the intent of the parties as derived from the facts and circumstances surrounding the issuance of the stock strongly supports the tax court's decision.

The securities were called preferred stock, were represented to everyone, including various regulatory bodies, as preferred stock, and were carried on the books of the company as preferred stock. Also, the seller's agent testified that it thought it was getting preferred stock, and this fact is of substantial weight for the petitioner insists that the seller devised the *type,* amount, and the basis upon which the securities would be issued.

In *Lee Telephone Co. v. Commissioner of Internal Revenue,* 260 F. 2d 114 (4th Cir. 1958), the court found a security to be an equity investment. Among its comments the court noted at pages 115–116:

> "Perhaps most important of all, the taxpayer, seeking to comply with applicable financial regulations, sought to place a preferred stock issue, to decrease rather than increase, the ratio of its debt to its net worth. The attorney for the taxpayer testified that at the time the taxpayer could have borrowed the money at 3 per cent, but the preferred stock was issued at the higher dividend rate because of the requirement of the regulatory commission. * * *"

The decision of the tax court will be affirmed on this point.

ACCOUNTING METHOD ISSUE

During the years 1953 to 1954 the petitioner operated approximately 1,000 vehicles. These vehicles were operated in excess of 33 million miles in each year and carried approximately 281 million passengers in 1953 and 250 million passengers in 1954. In 1953 petitioner's vehicles were involved in 5,903 accidents, and in 1954 there were 5,041 accidents.

Petitioner carried "excess public liability insurance" where liability occasioned by any one accident exceeded $100,000 and was less than $1,000,000, but was a self-insurer where liability was less than $100,-000. It maintained a staff of attorneys and claim adjusters to investigate accidents occurring in the course of the operation of its vehicles, to effect settlements, and to defend petitioner in suits brought by parties injured or damaged in such accidents. As of December 31, 1953, there were 414 claims unsettled which had arisen in that year, and as of December 31, 1954, there were 447 unsettled 1954 claims.

The tax court found as fact that:

> "At the end of each of the years 1953 and 1954, petitioner's board of directors appointed from their number, a committee of three (two of whom were attorneys) to examine the information gathered by petitioner's attorneys and claim adjusters relating to each of the unsettled claims, and to determine whether in such committee's opinion petitioner was liable, and to what extent. The committee members were assisted in their work for both taxable years, by the petitioner's general claim agent; and in the first of such years they were assisted also by a certified public accountant from the firm which audited petitioner's books of account."

This committee estimated that the petitioner's liability for the 414 unsettled 1953 claims was $254,-659. The estimate for the 447 unsettled 1954 claims was $161,136.50

The petitioner's general claims agent was in each year authorized to settle the pending claims at the amounts at which they had been appraised, but petitioner did not at any time notify or otherwise admit to any of the claimants that it considered itself liable.

In both years petitioner, an accrual basis taxpayer, set up on its books of account as a book liability for unsettled claims the above-mentioned estimates and also debited a related expense account for injuries and damages. On its Federal income tax return for 1953, it claimed a deduction of $254,659. In 1954, it claimed a deduction of $142,022.87 which was computed as follows:

Appraised liability on unsettled claims, 1954 accidents		$161,136.50
Deduct: Appraisal liability of 1953 claims settled in 1954	$94,984.00	
Less: Amounts at which 1953 claims were actually settled	75,870.37	19,113.63
Net amount expended and added to liability account		142,022.87

The respondent, in his statutory notices of deficiency, disallowed the entire amount of $254,659 which was claimed as a deduction on petitioner's 1953 return, and he also disallowed $61,472.79 of the $142,022.87 which was claimed as a deduction on petitioner's 1954 return. The respondent allowed as a deduction in each taxable year the amount of the claims for injuries and damages which actually were settled by the petitioner in each such year.

A substantial number of the unsettled claims for 1953 and 1954 were put into litigation either before or after the close of the taxable year concerned. In all litigated claims the petitioner denied liability in its pleadings. There also was a large number of potential claims which never progressed beyond the point of reports made to petitioner by its employees for the injured parties neither presented claims to petitioner nor filed suit against it.

There were in the two year span 64 claims where the petitioner's committee determined that the petitioner had no liability. Ultimately, however, in 57 of these claims some settlement was made with the claimants.

The tax court further found that:

> "As regards claims wherein the committee had estimated that petitioner was liable and settlements were made (either with or without litigaton), the settlement amounts were equal to the estimates in only 31 out of 261 of such 1953 claims, and in only 22 out of 254 of such claims. Settlements were at variance with estimates by more than 100 percent in 97 of said 1953 claims and in 102 of said 1954 claims."

As of the time of trial, there were still 8 unsettled 1953 claims where liability was currently estimated at $14,500, although the original estimate was $5,200. In addition, there were 13 unsettled 1954 claims currently estimated at $51,415 and originally estimated at $12,750.

The tax court included in its findings the following table which compares petitioner's estimates with its actual experience:

Year	Number of claims	Petitioner's estimated liability	Payments actually made in settlement of same, through Aug. 31, 1958
1953	414	*$254,659.00	$173,230.24
1954	447	**161,136.50	159,851.84

*Includes $34,470, representing 138 unpressed claims.
**Includes $26,521, representing 124 unpressed claims.

As the tax court stated:

> "The question here presented is whether petioner, an accrual basis taxpayer, may deduct for each of the years 1953 and 1954, certain amounts accrued by it on its books of account as of December 31 of each year. Such amounts represented its estimate of the probable amounts which it would have to pay in settlement for personal injuries and property damages, arising out of accidents in which its employees and equipment were involved."

The tax court decided that the aforementioned estimates were not deductible on two grounds. One such ground was that the unsettled claims did not represent fixed liabilities during the year in which the deduction was claimed because some claims were being litigated, and as to all other liability was not admitted. In other words, all claims were contested. The other reason was that the amount of liability was not ascertainable with reasonable certainty. This was based on the fact that as to individual claims, the estimates were very often at variance with the actual settlements, settlements were made in many cases where a determination of nonliability had been made, and many claims were in effect only potential claims which were in fact never pressed.

As mentioned above, the petitioner keeps its books on an accrual basis. Section 446 of the 1954 Internal Revenue Code requires the petitioner to compute its income under the method of accounting used in keeping its books unless such method does not clearly reflect income. In the instant case, it is the opinion of the court that petitioner's method of accruing its estimated liability does not clearly reflect its income on an annual basis.

In *United States* v. *Anderson*, 269 U.S. 422 (1926), the court, when speaking of the purpose of comparable provisions of the earlier Revenue Code, stated at page 440:

> "* * * It was to enable taxpayers to keep their books and make their returns according to scientific accounting principles, by charging against income earned during the taxable period, the expenses incurred in and properly attributable to the process of earning income during that period; * * *."

The reasoning of the court in *United States* v. *Anderson* is equally applicable to the case at bar for there is no question but that the expenses resulting from the various claims are chargeable to the income of the year in which the accident happened. During the trial petitioner produced expert witnesses who testified to the effect that petitioner's procedures were in keeping with generally accepted accounting principles.

While an expense may be logically related to one year or another, it is true that to be deductible as an accrual all events which establish a definite liability in the taxpayer must have occurred during the taxable year, and the amount of such liability must be determinable with reasonable certainty. *Dixie Pine Products Co.* v. *Commissioner of Internal Revenue,* 320 U.S. 516 (1944); *United States* v. *Anderson,* 269 U.S. 422 (1926). In the instant case, the court feels that these tests have been met by the petitioner.

The petitioner argues, and rightly so, that all events which determine liability have occurred. The accidents out of which the various claims grow undoubtedly have occurred in the years in question, and the physical facts of the accidents are the only events upon which liability is predicated. Although it is true that the petitioner could not have known the full extent of personal injuries in 1953 or 1954 in any particular case, still this has no bearing on liability itself, but instead is concerned with the question of whether an admitted liability is sufficiently fixed.

In this case then, we have a situation where the operative facts have actually occurred although their meaning or even existence are subject to argument. This is in contrast to the situation where the operative facts have not occurred but are highly predictable. In the latter situation, many businesses prudently set up reserves to protect themselves, but they are not deductible as accrued expenses for although intimately related to the income of the earlier year, the events which fix liability have not happened. This is true even though the future expenses are predictable with great accuracy. *Brown v. Helvering,* 291 U.S. 193 (1934). In the instant case, the expense is related to the income of the earlier year, and the operative facts upon which liability is dependent have occurred.

As mentioned previously, one reason for the tax court's refusal to allow a deduction in this case was the fact that some claims were being litigated, and liability was not admitted by petitioner as to the rest. Normally it is true that a contested claim is not deductible. *Security Flour Mills Co. v. Commissioner of Internal Revenue,* 321 U.S. 281 (1944); *Dixie Pine Products Co. v. Commissioner of Internal Revenue,* 320 U.S. 516 (1944); and *Lucas v. American Code Co., Inc.,* 280 U.S. 445 (1930).

In all the above-cited cases, there was only a single claim being contested. In such a situation, it is obvious that (1) there may or may not be liability depending on the outcome of the contest, and (2) the amount of the liability is quite often uncertain.

In the present situation there are numerous claims, and assuming at this point that in the aggregate the amount of liability is predictable, neither of the above reasons for not allowing a deduction is pertinent. In the first place, although all claims are contested, this is not a situation where there may or may not be liability, depending on the outcome of the contest. Because of the number of claims, it is apparent to everyone that there is going to be liability, and the only question is in which particular claims this liability will occur. The same line of reasoning applies to the objection that the amount of liability is dependent on the contest. If overall liability can be accurately predicted, there should not be any objection to the fact that it cannot be tied down securely in any particular claim.

In *Ocean Accident & Guarantee Corp., Ltd. v. Commissioner of Internal Revenue*, 47 F. 2d 582 (2d Cir. 1931), a case directly in point, the court stated at page 584:

"This brings us to the question whether the deduction claimed by petitioner was an 'accrued' loss. It was an aggregate of estimates of policy losses likely to be suffered on account of all accidents or injuries reported to petitioner during the taxable year. As to some cases, the petitioner may have admitted liability in the amount of the estimate set up on its record card, and so might come within the terms of Article III of Regulations No. 45 as to a deductible loss under clause (4) of section 234(a). But most of the estimates of liability were not of that character. Each one, viewed alone, would be too contingent as to payment and too uncertain as to amount to be deductible as a 'loss sustained.' *Lucas v. Am. Code Co.,* 280 U.S. 445, 50 S. Ct. 202, 203, 74 L. Ed. 538. But the question is whether the aggregate of estimated unpaid losses for any year may not be taken as an aggregate of accrued losses, though each one separately, or at least most of them, would be contingent and unpredictable. The business of insurance presupposes that the insurer is able to treat as accurately computable and predictable an aggregate of variables no one of which is either computable or predictable. Without that the business must fail, and only past experience permits any estimate as to the extent to which the variations cancel each other. But the business does go on and with a certainty greater than most others. Here the accrued losses were predictable with remarkable accuracy, the business of petitioner being large enough to disregard the contingencies inherent in each loss taken alone. *To assimilate such a situation to a single loss is, in our opinion, to close one's eyes to the substance of the business.* We do not think the American Code Case so requires. * * *" [Emphasis added.]

The tax court was of the opinion that regardless of the question of a definite fixed liability, the expenses involved in this case could not be estimated with any reasonable certainty. Basically this view was bottomed on the fact that individually the claims were quite difficult to evaluate, and in many cases actual settlement figures differed radically from the estimates made. This view ignores the fact that in the aggregate the unsettled claims are susceptible of reasonably accurate estimation as was recognized in the *Ocean Accident* decision, *supra*.

A comparison of the petitioner's aggregate estimates with actual settlement figures for the years 1953 and 1954 follows:

1953 Estimate—$254,659.00
Cost of 1953 cases settled	$178, 230. 24
Current estimate of unsettled cases	14, 500. 00
Total	192, 730. 24

1954 Estimate—$161,136.50
Cost of 1954 cases settled	$159, 851. 84
Current estimate of unsettled cases	51, 415. 00
Total	211, 266. 84

While it is apparent from these figures that petitioner was not able to estimate its liability with mathematical precision, this need not deter the deduction for it is only necessary that the estimate be reasonably certain. *Harrold* v. *Commissioner of Internal Revenue*, 192 F. 2d 1002 (4th Cir. 1951); *Denise Coal Co.* v. *Commissioner of Internal Revenue*, 271 F. 2d 930 (3rd Cir. 1959); and *Hilinski* v. *Commissioner of Internal Revenue*, 237 F. 2d 703 (6th Cir. 1956).

For example, a deduction was allowed in the *Harrold* case although the expense which was estimated at $31,090 was covered by an actual expenditure of only $25,210.18. See also *Patsch* v. *Commissioner of Internal Revenue*, 208 F. 2d 532 (3rd Cir. 1953), which specifically approved this holding of the *Harrold* decision, and *Denise Coal Co.* v. *Commissioner of Internal Revenue, supra.*

Under the circumstances of this case, the court is of the opinion that a reasonably certain estimate was made with due regard for the actual facts and conditions underlying each claim. The estimates here were made in good faith during the early period of the petitioner's corporate existence, were carefully considered, and can in no way be equated with the arbitrary figures used by the taxpayer in *Patsch* v. *Commissioner of Internal Revenue, supra.* Also of some interest is the fact that when the two years of 1953 and 1954 are considered together, the petitioner's estimates are accurate to within 2.9 percent.

The volume of accidents here involved is substantial. It is probably as substantial as that of a small insurance company. The volume is sufficient so that the overall reserve can be fixed with reasonable accuracy notwithstanding the fact that as to any one case, claim, or potential claim it may not be accurate. With this volume of accidents, the total liability can be predicted with reasonable certainty as to any one year. Where such volume exists, it is the opinion of the court that the taxpayer is justified in following the standard accounting practices for this type of operation. There is no intimation here that the taxpayer was endeavoring to accomplish any illegitimate purpose with reference to the deduction for its estimated liability.

The decision of the tax court is reversed on this point.

A true Copy:

Teste:

_____

*Clerk of the United States Court of
Appeals for the Seventh Circuit.*

UNITED STATES COURT OF APPEALS FOR THE SEVENTH
CIRCUIT

_____

Monday, October 24, 1960

Before Hon. F. RYAN DUFFY, *Circuit Judge*; Hon. WIN G. KNOCH, *Circuit Judge*; Hon. KENNETH P. GRUBB, *District Judge.*

No. 13025

MILWAUKEE & SUBURBAN TRANSPORT CORPORATION,
PETITIONER

vs.

COMMISSIONER OF INTERNAL REVENUE, RESPONDENT

PETITION FOR REVIEW OF A DECISION OF THE TAX COURT
OF THE UNITED STATES

This cause came on to be heard on the transcript of the record from the Tax Court of the United States, and was argued by counsel.

61

On consideration whereof, it is ordered and adjudged by this Court that the decision of the Tax Court of the United States entered in this cause on November 19, 1959, be, and the same is hereby, AFFIRMED on the Preferred Stock issue, and REVERSED on the Accounting Method issue, in accordance with the opinion of this Court filed this day.

A True Copy:
Teste:

KENNETH J. CARRICK,
Clerk of the United States Court of
Appeals for the Seventh Circuit.

APPENDIX B

Internal Revenue Code of 1939:

SEC. 22. GROSS INCOME.

(a) *General Definition.*—"Gross income" includes gains, profits, and income derived from salaries, wages, or compensation for personal service, of whatever kind and in whatever form paid, or from professions, vocations, trades, businesses, commerce, or sales, or dealings in property, whether real or personal, growing out of the ownership or use of or interest in such property; also from interest, rent, dividends, securities, or the transaction of any business carried on for gain or profit, or gains or profits and income derived from any source whatever. * * *

*   *   *   *   *

(26 U.S.C. 1952 ed., Sec. 22.)

SEC. 23. DEDUCTIONS FROM GROSS INCOME.

In computing net income there shall be allowed as deductions:

(a) [As amended by Sec. 121(a), Revenue Act of 1942, c. 619, 56 Stat. 798] *Expenses.*—

(1) *Trade or business expenses.—*

(A) *In General.*—All the ordinary and necessary expenses paid or incurred during the taxable year in carrying on any trade or business, including a reasonable allowance for salaries or other compensation for personal services actually rendered; * * * and rentals or other payments required to be made as a condition to the continued use or possession, for purposes of the trade or business, of property to which the taxpayer has not taken or is not taking title or in which he has no equity.

*   *   *   *   *

(26 U.S.C. 1952 ed., Sec. 23.)

SEC. 41. GENERAL RULE.

The net income shall be computed upon the basis of the taxpayer's annual accounting period (fiscal year or calendar year, as the case may be) in accordance with the method of accounting regularly employed in keeping the books of such taxpayer; but if no such method of accounting has been so employed, or if the method employed does not clearly reflect the income, the computation shall be made in accordance with such method as in the opinion of the Commissioner does clearly reflect the income. If the taxpayer's annual accounting period is other than a fiscal year as defined in section 48 or if the taxpayer has no annual accounting period or does not keep books, the net income shall be computed on the basis of the calendar year.

(26 U.S.C. 1952 ed., Sec. 41.)

SEC. 42 [As amended by Sec. 114, Revenue Act of 1941, c. 412, 55 Stat. 687]. PERIOD IN WHICH ITEMS OF GROSS INCOME INCLUDED.

(a) *General Rule.*—The amount of all items of gross income shall be included in the gross income for the taxable year in which received by the taxpayer, unless, under methods of accounting permitted under section 41, any such amounts are to be properly accounted for as of a different period. * * *

* * * * *

(26 U.S.C. 1952 ed., Sec. 42.)

SEC. 43. PERIOD FOR WHICH DEDUCTIONS AND CREDITS TAKEN.

The deductions and credits (other than the corporation dividends paid credit provided in section 27) provided for in this chapter shall be taken for the taxable year in which "paid or accrued" or "paid or incurred", dependent upon the method of accounting upon the basis of which the net income is computed, unless in order to clearly reflect the income the deductions or credits should be taken as of a different period. * * *

(26 U.S.C. 1952 ed., Sec. 43.)

Sections 61, 162, 446(a), (b) and (c), 451 and 461 of the Internal Revenue Code of 1954, applicable to the year 1954, while more explicit, are in all material respects substantially the same as the sections set out above.

Treasury Regulations 118 (1939 Code):

SEC. 39.41-1. *Computation of net income.* Net income must be computed with respect to a fixed period. Usually that period is 12 months and is known as the taxable year. Items of income and of expenditure which as gross income and deductions are elements in the computation of net income need not be in the form of cash. It is sufficient that such items, if otherwise properly included in the computation, can be valued in terms of money. The time as of which any item of gross income or any deduction is to be accounted for must be determined in the light of the fundamental rule that the computation shall be made in such a manner as clearly reflects the taxpayer's income. If the method of accounting regularly employed by him in keeping his books clearly reflects his income, it is to be followed with respect to the time as of which items of gross income and deductions are to be accounted for. (See Sections 39.42–1 to 39.42–3, inclusive.) If the taxpayer does not regularly employ a method of accounting which clearly reflects his income, the computation shall be made in such manner as in the opinion of the Commissioner clearly reflects it.

SEC. 39.41–2. *Bases of computation and changes in accounting methods.* (a) Approved standard methods of accounting will ordinarily be regarded as clearly reflecting income. A method of accounting will not, however, be regarded as clearly reflecting income unless all items of gross income and all deductions are treated with reasonable consistency. See Section 48 for definitions of "paid or accrued" and "paid or incurred." All items of gross income shall be included in the gross income for the taxable year in which they are received by the taxpayer, and deductions taken accordingly, unless in order clearly to reflect income such amounts are to be properly accounted for as of a different period. But see sections 42 and 43. See also section 48. For instance, in any case in which it is necessary to use an inventory, no method of accounting in regard to purchases and sales will correctly reflect income except an accrual method. A taxpayer is deemed to have received items of gross income which have been credited to or set apart for him without restriction. (See sections 39.42–2 and 39.42–3.) On the other hand, appreciation in value of property is not even an accrual of income to a taxpayer prior to the realization of such appreciation through sale or conversion of the property. (But see section 39.22(c)–5.)

*   *   *   *   *

SEC. 39.42–1. *When included in gross income.*—(a) *In general.*—Except as otherwise provided in section 42, gains, profits, and income are to be included in the gross income for the taxable year in which they are received by the taxpayer, unless they are included as of a different period in accordance with the approved method of accounting followed by him. See Sections 39.41–1 to 39.41–3, inclusive. * * *

*   *   *   *   *

SEC. 39.43–1. *"Paid or incurred" and "paid or accrued."* (a) The terms "paid or incurred" and "paid or accrued" will be construed according to the method of accounting upon the basis of which the net income is computed by the taxpayer. (See section 48(c).) The deductions and credits provided for in chapter 1 (other than the dividends paid credit provided in section 27) must be taken for the taxable year in which "paid or accrued" or "paid or incurred," unless in order clearly to reflect the income such deductions or credits should be taken as of a different period. If a taxpayer desires to claim a deduction or a credit as of a period other than the period in which it was "paid or accrued" or "paid or incurred," he shall attach to his return a statement setting forth his request for consideration of the case by the Commissioner together with a complete statement of the facts upon which he relies. However, in his income tax return he shall take the deduction or credit only for the taxable period in which it was actually "paid or incurred," or "paid or accrued," as the case may be. Upon the audit of the return, the Commissioner will decide whether the case is within the exception provided by the Internal Revenue Code, and the taxpayer will be advised as to the period for which the deduction or credit is properly allowable.

* * * * *

SEC. 39.43-2. *When charges deductible.* Each year's return, so far as practicable, both as to gross income and deductions therefrom, should be complete in itself, and taxpayers are expected to make every reasonable effort to ascertain the facts necessary to make a correct return. The expenses, liabilities, or deficit of one year cannot be used to reduce the income of a subsequent year. A taxpayer has the right to deduct all authorized allowances, and it follows that if he does not within any year deduct certain of his expenses, losses, interest, taxes, or other charges, he cannot deduct them from the income of the next or any succeeding year. It is recognized, however, that particularly in a growing business of any magnitude there are certain overlapping items both of income and deduction, and so long as these overlapping items do not materially distort the income they may be included in the year in which the taxpayer, pursuant to a consistent policy, takes them into his accounts. * * *

Sections 1.441-1 (a) to (e), 1.446-1 (a) to (c) and 1.451-1(a), Treasury Regulations on Income Tax (1954 Code), while more explicit, are in all material respects substantially the same as the sections set out above.

U.S. GOVERNMENT PRINTING OFFICE, 1961

IN THE

Supreme Court of the United States

OCTOBER TERM, 1960.

No. 843

COMMISSIONER OF INTERNAL REVENUE,
Petitioner,

vs.

MILWAUKEE & SUBURBAN TRANSPORT
CORPORATION,
Respondent.

ON PETITION FOR A WRIT OF CERTIORARI TO THE UNITED STATES
COURT OF APPEALS FOR THE SEVENTH CIRCUIT.

BRIEF FOR RESPONDENT IN OPPOSITION.

RICHARD R. TESCHNER,
ROBERT THORSEN,
WARREN W. BROWNING,
DALE L. SORDEN,
411 East Mason Street,
Milwaukee 2, Wisconsin,
Counsel for Respondent.

QUARLES, HERRIOTT & CLEMONS,
Milwaukee, Wisconsin.

MADIGAN AND THORSEN,
Chicago, Illinois.

BROWNING & BROWNING,
Chicago, Illinois.

THE GUNTHORP-WARREN PRINTING COMPANY, CHICAGO

INDEX.

CITATIONS.

Cases.

iii

Statutes.

Miscellaneous.

Supreme Court of the United States

OCTOBER TERM, 1960.

NO. 843.

COMMISSIONER OF INTERNAL REVENUE,
Petitioner,

vs.

MILWAUKEE & SUBURBAN TRANSPORT CORPORATION,

Respondent.

ON PETITION FOR A WRIT OF CERTIORARI TO THE UNITED STATES COURT OF APPEALS FOR THE SEVENTH CIRCUIT.

BRIEF FOR RESPONDENT IN OPPOSITION.

OPINIONS BELOW.

The memorandum opinion of the Tax Court (App. A of Petition pp. 10-41), T. C. Memo 1959-216, is not officially reported. Unofficial reports are found at 18 TCM 1039 and 1959 P-H TC Memo Dec. ¶ 59,216. The opinion of the Court of Appeals (App. A of Petition pp. 42-60) is reported at 283 F. 2d 279.

The printing of the opinion of the Court of Appeals in Appendix A of the Petition contains a confusing typographical error. At page 54, the fourth line from the bottom, the word "not" should be deleted. Corrected, the phrase reads, "it is the opinion of the court that petitioner's method of accruing its estimated liability does clearly reflect its income on an annual basis."

QUESTION PRESENTED.

The taxpayer, a municipal transit company filing its federal income tax returns on an accrual basis, regularly employs in keeping its books a generally accepted method of accounting, standard in its industry, which involves accruing each year the estimated amount of incurred liability for injuries and damages arising out of accidents which occurred that year but were unsettled as of the close of the year. As claims are disposed of in subsequent years any net difference between estimated and settled liability is taken into account in the year of disposition.

The Circuit Court of Appeals in its decision quoted with approval the statement of the question set out by the Tax Court: It is as follows:

> "The question here presented is whether petitioner, an accrual basis taxpayer, may deduct for each of the years 1953 and 1954, certain amounts accrued by it on its books of account as of December 31 of each year. Such amounts represented its estimate of the probable amounts which it would have to pay in settlement for personal injuries and property damages, arising out of accidents in which its employees and equipment were involved."

For reasons of its own, the Government chose to alter that question.

STATUTES AND REGULATIONS INVOLVED.

The pertinent provisions of the Internal Revenue Code of 1939 and Treasury Regulations thereunder are printed in Appendix B of the Petition, pp. 61-66. The pertinent provisions of Sections 162, 446 and 461 of the Internal Revenue Code of 1954 and Sections 1.446-1 and 1.461-1, Treasury Regulations on Income Tax (1954 Code), are printed in an Appendix C appended hereto.

STATEMENT.

This case does not, as the Government states (Petition pp. 2, 4, 6, 8), involve an addition to a "reserve"; it involves accrual of the estimated amount of liabilities already incurred although not yet settled. Historically, in the decisions of this and other courts, the difference has been critical. The two situations ought not be confused. It is therefore necessary to restate the facts.

The taxpayer, a Wisconsin corporation, operates the transit system in and around Milwaukee, which it acquired by purchase of assets on December 30, 1952. It files its returns on a calendar year and accrual basis. During 1953 and 1954, it operated approximately 1,000 vehicles, carrying from 250 to 281 million passengers annually. Its vehicles were involved in 5,903 accidents in 1953 and 5,041 accidents in 1954. (Petition p. 2; Pet. App. A pp. 20, 43, 50-51.)

So far as here material taxpayer was a self-insurer of its accident liabilities. It maintained a staff of attorneys and claims adjusters to investigate, settle and defend claims for personal injuries and property damages. As of December 31, 1953, there were 414 unsettled claims from accidents occurring in that year; at the end of 1954 there were 447 unsettled claims arising out of accidents in that year. (Petition pp. 2-3.)

At the end of each year, taxpayer's Board of Directors appointed from their number a committee of three (two of whom were attorneys) to examine the information gathered by its attorneys and claims adjusters relating to each of the unsettled claims. The committee made an appraisal or estimate of the amount for which, in their opinion, the taxpayer was liable, if at all, in each instance. The total estimated amount was set up on the taxpayer's books of account as a book liability for unsettled claims for injuries and damages. This amount was $254,659 for 1953 and

$161,136.50 for 1954. (Petition p. 3; Pet. App. A pp. 31, 51.)

Taxpayer's general claims agent was in each year authorized to settle the pending claims at the amounts at which they had been appraised, but taxpayer did not at any time notify or otherwise admit to any of the claimants that it considered itself liable. The appraised estimates were kept confidential and taxpayer's agents tried to settle claims at the lowest possible figure. (Petition pp. 3-4.)

The aggregate estimated liability so determined was accrued on taxpayer's books as an expense and a liability at the end of each fiscal year. As payments were made in future years in settlement of these liabilities, the amount thereof was charged to the accrued liability and was not charged to expense in the year of settlement. Accidents were considered settled when agreement was reached with the injured person, or upon conclusion of any litigation, or if no claim was filed within the two year statute of limitations applicable under local law. Any net difference between liability as appraised and as finally determined was reflected in book and taxable income in the year of settlement.[1] (Petition App. A pp. 32, 42; R. 110, 113.)

Taxpayer's method of accounting for its liabilities for injuries and damages unsettled at the close of the year in which the accidents occur is in accordance with generally accepted principles of accrual accounting, has been consistently applied by the taxpayer since it first commenced business and is the recognized and accepted method of accounting for such liabilities in the transit industry. (Petition App. A p. 55; R. 103-104, 107.)

In filing its federal income tax returns taxpayer accounted for its injuries and damages liabilities unsettled

1. This method of adjusting such differences is specifically required and authorized by Treasury Regulations Sec. 1.461-1 (a) (2). (Appendix C, *infra*, pp. 23-24.)

at the close of the year in which the accident occurred in accordance with the same method which it used to compute its income in keeping its books. The resulting deductions were $254,659 for 1953 and $142,028.87 for 1954, the latter figure computed as follows (Petition p. 5; Petition App. A pp. 32, 52):

Appraised liability on unsettled claims,
1954 accidents $161,136.50
Deduct: Appraised liability of
1953 claims settled in 1954...$94,984.00
Less: Amounts at which 1953
claims were actually settled.. 75,870.37
                                                    ――――――   19,113.63

Net amount expensed and added to liability account, 1954.................... $142,022.87

At the time of trial all but 8 of the 1953 claims and all but 13 of the 1954 claims had been settled. According to the best evidence available at time of trial, taxpayer's liability on unsettled 1953 claims (originally estimated at $5,200) was $14,500 and its liability on unsettled 1954 claims (originally estimated at $12,750) was $51,415. (Petition p. 4; Petition Exhibit A pp. 35, 53; R. 87-89.)[2]

The Commissioner disallowed the entire amount of $254,659 deducted by taxpayer in 1953 and $61,472.79 of the $142,022.87 deducted by taxpayer in 1954 under its method of accounting for these liabilities. The Commissioner allowed as a deduction only the amount of these claims which were actually settled or paid in each year, namely, none in 1953 and $80,530.08 in 1954. (Petition p. 5; Pet. App. pp. 32-33, 52.)

_____

2. The revised estimate figures stated in the Tax Court opinion and quoted by the Court of Appeals differ from the figures stated here and in the testimony by $3,500 in 1953 and $1,000 in 1954 because of one case in each year pending at date of trial but not appraised at the close of the accident year. R. 87-89.

...Viewing each claim separately, taxpayer's estimates of liability varied substantially from the liability finally determined. (Petition p. 4.) However, viewed in the aggregate, taxpayer's actual liability (actual settlements plus currently revised estimates of the few remaining unsettled claims) compares with the deduction claimed by taxpayer under its method of accounting and with the deduction allowed by the Commissioner as follows (Petition pp. 4, 5; Petition App. A pp. 32, 35, 36, 52, 53; R. 87-89; See also Footnote 2, p. 5):

	Actual Liability	Taxpayer's Deduction	% to Actual	Commr's. Deduction	% to Actual
1953	$196,230.24	$254,359.00	130%	—0—	00%
1954	212,266.84	142,022.87	67%	$80,550.08[3]	38%
Total	$408,497.08	$396,681.87	97%	$80,550.08	20%

A comparison of the accuracy of the respondent's method with that contended for by the Commissioner thus indicates that while the respondent's method results in a determination which was 97% of the final determination, the Commissioner's method results in a determination which is only 20% correct when measured against the final liability.

The Tax Court sustained the Commissioner. (Petition App. A pp. 36-41.) The Court of Appeals reversed. (Petition App. A pp. 50-60.)

---

3. The difference between the 1954 settlements of 1953 cases ($75,870.37) and the deduction allowed by the Commissioner ($80,550.08) is not explained by the record. It is apparently attributable to payments in 1954 in partial satisfaction of liability on 1953 accidents (medical expenses, etc.) in cases where total liability was not settled until a later year.

SUMMARY OF ARGUMENT.

Respondent opposes the granting of a petition for certiorari in this case for the following reasons:

(1) The decision of the court below is limited to an almost unique set of facts, has no general application, and does not involve an important question of federal law.

(2) The decision is not in conflict with the decision of any other circuit, nor does it conflict with any decision of the Seventh Circuit.

(3) The decision does not conflict with any applicable decisions of this Court; as a matter of fact it follows the applicable decisions of this Court.

(4) The question presented in this case is not related to questions involved in the two cases referred to as awaiting argument in this Court (*American Automobile Association* v. *United States*, No. 288; and *United States* v. *Consolidated Edison Co. of New York*, No. 357).

(5) The decision of the court below is not in derogation of the annual accounting rule but is an excellent exemplification of that rule.

(6) The reference in the Government's petition to the now repealed Section 462 of the Internal Revenue Code of 1954 indicates a misconception of the issue presented herein, and the obvious distinction between that issue and the section cited.

ARGUMENT IN OPPOSITION TO GRANTING THE WRIT.

The holding of the Court of Appeals in this case is extremely limited and depends on a conjunction of facts far too unusual to warrant review by this Court on certiorari. Not except by gross generalization may the issues in this case be related to the issues in the two cases cited by petitioner in which certiorari has been granted and the

8

four in which petitions are pending. All involve the broad topic of accounting methods but no holding in those cases is likely to have application to this one, or vice versa.

So far as has been disclosed by the briefing of both parties in both courts below, this case presents a factual situation which has been the subject of reported tax dispute only once before since the beginning of the income tax law. That was 30 years ago in *Ocean Accident & G. Corp.* v. *Commissioner*, 47 F. 2d 582 (CA 2, 1931), dealing with the years 1918-1920.[4]

The peculiar factors involved in the present case are:

(1) the deduction of an aggregate of estimates of liabilities already incurred (as distinguished from a reserve based on prediction of liabilities likely to be incurred in the future),

(2) where the number of items making up the aggregate is sufficiently large to permit of a reasonable estimate of the aggregate despite the uncertainties inherent in each item taken alone,

(3) where it is established that such is a generally accepted method of accounting for such items, standard in the industry involved, on the basis of which the taxpayer regularly computes its income in keeping its books, and

(4) where no *change* of accounting method is in-

4. Commencing with the next year, 1921, insurance companies have deducted such liabilities under special statutory provisions which have eliminated any need for further testing by them of the general statutory provisions applicable here and in *Ocean Accident*. Section 246 (b) (6) of the Revenue Act of 1921, continued as Section 204 (b) (6) of the Internal Revenue Code of 1939 and as Section 832 (b) (5) (B) of the Internal Revenue Code of 1954. Contrary to the statement in the petition (Petition pp. 4-5) *Ocean Accident* did not turn on provisions peculiar to insurance companies but rather presented a pure question of accrual identical to the one here presented. See pp. 18-19 hereof.

volved. (Thus the Commissioner's plenary power to
consent or not, to accounting method *changes*, is not
involved.)

No reported case, other than this one and *Ocean Accident*,
presents such a situation. The group of accounting method
cases now pending before this Court present distinctly
different facts and questions. Petitioner has made no
showing of even one case now pending anywhere in the
United States involving the same or even closely similar
facts and circumstances. Respondent knows of none. Only
two such cases have been litigated since the excise (income)
tax levied upon corporations by the Act of August 5, 1909
(36 Stat. 113). Two Courts of Appeals have passed on
the question. Their decisions are in perfect harmony, not
in conflict. The mere possibility that a similar situation
may perhaps arise sometime in the next thirty or forty
years is scarcely enough to convert the dispute between
these present litigants into an important question of federal
law which demands decision by this Court.

THERE IS NO CONFLICT WITH PRIOR DECISIONS OF THIS COURT.

Petitioner claims conflict with *Security Mills Co.* v. *Commissioner*, 321 U. S. 281 (1944); *Dixie Pine Products Co.* v.
Commissioner, 320 U. S. 516 (1944); and *Lucas* v. *American
Code Co., Inc.*, 280 U. S. 445 (1930). There is no conflict.
The two Courts of Appeals involved have merely declined
to extend the rule of these cases beyond its reason. With
reference to these three cases the Seventh Circuit in the
instant case said:

"In all the above-cited cases, there was only a single
claim being contested. In such a situation, it is obvious that (1) there may or may not be liability depending on the outcome of the contest, and (2) the amount
of the liability is quite often uncertain.

"In the present situation there are numerous claims,

and assuming at this point that in the aggregate the amount of liability is predictable, neither of the above reasons for not allowing a deduction is pertinent. * * * this is not a situation where there may or may not be liability, depending on the outcome of the contest. * * * If overall liability can be accurately predicted, there should not be any objection to the fact that it cannot be tied down securely in any particular claim.'' (Petition Appendix A, pp. 56-57; 283 F. 2d 279, 286-287.)

The Second Circuit reasoned similarly in *Ocean Accident & G. Corp.* v. *Commissioner*, 47 F. 2d 582, 584.

"Each one, viewed alone, would be too contingent as to payment and too uncertain as to amount to be deductible as a 'loss sustained.' *Lucas* v. *Am. Code Co.*, 280 U. S. 445, 50 S. Ct. 202, 203, 74 L. Ed. 538. But the question is whether the aggregate of estimated unpaid losses for any year may not be taken as an aggregate of accrued losses, though each one separately, or at least most of them, would be contingent and unpredictable. * * * Here the accrued losses were predictable with remarkable accuracy, the business of petitioner being large enough to disregard the contingencies inherent in each loss taken alone. To assimilate such a situation to a single loss is, in our opinion, to close one's eyes to the substance of the business. We do not think the American Code Case so requires.''

Petitioner also cites as in conflict *Brown* v. *Helvering*, 291 U. S. 193 and *U. S.* v. *Anderson*, 269 U. S. 422. To the contrary, the difference between those two cases, and the reasoning of both of them, illustrates exactly why the instant case involves a deductible accrual rather than a nondeductible reserve. The question in *Anderson* was whether an accrual basis taxpayer ought to deduct its 1916 munitions tax in 1916, as the Government there contended, or in 1917 when it was settled and paid. In deciding for deduction in the earlier year, this Court laid down the famous "all events" test.

"In a technical legal sense it may be argued that a tax does not accrue until it has been assessed and become due; but it is also true that in advance of the assessment of a tax, all the events may occur which fix the amount of the tax and determine the liability of the taxpayer to pay it. In this respect, for purposes of accounting and of ascertaining true income for a given accounting period, the munitions tax here in question did not stand on any different footing than other accrued expenses appearing on appellee's books." (269 U. S. 422, 441.)

It was perfectly clear in the context of the case that this Court was there talking about a situation in which the operative facts have actually occurred although their meaning or even existence may be subject to future argument; that it is *not* required that the *determination* of liability shall have occurred; that what *is* required is that the *events* shall have occurred *from which* the liability is determined.

"By the close of the year, liability for the tax had become definitely fixed, the tax being based on the result of operations for 1916 * * * neither liability for the tax nor the amount properly payable could be affected under the law by anything occurring after December 31, 1916. * * * The fact that a difference of opinion might arise after December 31, 1916, between the taxpayer and the Commissioner of Internal Revenue as to what was a reasonable depreciation on plant and equipment, or as to other items of that nature, did not provide new factors occurring after December 31, 1916, varying the tax." 269 U. S. 422, 425-426 (Argument for the United States).

"A consideration of the difficulties involved in the preparation of an income account on a strict basis of receipts and disbursements * * * indicates with no uncertainty the purpose of Sections 12(a) and 13(d) [§§ 446, 1954 Code] * * * to enable taxpayers to keep their books and make their returns according to scientific accounting principles, by charging against income earned during the taxable period, the expenses incurred in and properly attributable to the process of earning income during that period * * *.

"The appellee's true income * * * could not have been determined without deducting from its gross income for the year the total cost and expenses attributable to the production of that income during the year." 269 U. S. 422, 440 (Opinion of the Court).

That the crucial question is the occurrence of the *events* which determine liability, not the determination itself, accords with the Government's own historical and never revoked position, I. T. 2500, VIII-2 CB 103 (1929), and has recently been expressly reaffirmed by this Court. *Lewyt Corp.* v. *Commissioner,* 349 U. S. 237, 243.

Brown v. *Helvering,* 291 U. S. 193, illustrates the distinctly different situation of an attempt to deduct a reserve against liability which will arise from the occurrence of events in the future—there, cancellation of policies. The distinction is not in the degree of certainty but rather in the time of occurrence of the operative facts. Mr. Brown was attempting to predict how many of his policyholders *would* cancel in the future; but they had not done so yet, whereas the events giving rise to the munitions tax liability in *Anderson* and the traffic accidents giving rise to the taxpayer's injuries and damages liabilities in this case had indisputably occurred prior to the end of the years in question beyond man's power to change them.

There is a further distinction between the instant decision and *Brown* v. *Helvering,* in that the *Brown* case involved a *change* of accounting method from that employed in previous years. In such situations the plenary power of the Commissioner to accept or reject the change is well known and statutory (§ 446 (e) IRC 1954).

"The accrual method of accounting had been regularly

employed by Edward Brown & Sons before 1923, but no 'return commissions' account had been set up * * *. In assessing the deficiencies, the Commissioner required in effect that the taxpayer continue to follow the method of accounting which had been in use prior to the change made in 1923. To do so was within his administrative discretion * * * 291 U. S. 193, 203.

"This proposed alternative method of computing the income * * * was not employed * * * either before or after 1923. * * * The Commissioner was of opinion that the method of accounting consistently applied prior to 1923 accurately reflected the income. He was vested with a wide discretion in deciding whether to permit or to forbid a change." 291 U. S. 193, 204.

Several courts of appeals have recently indicated their belief that this "change of accounting method" feature of *Brown* is its true teaching. *Bressner Radio, Inc. v. Commissioner*, 267 F. 2d 520, 523; *Beacon Publishing Co. v. Commissioner*, 218 F. 2d 697, 701, cf. 702.

THERE IS NO CONFLICT WITH DECISIONS OF OTHER CIRCUITS.

The Petition also asserts, although with neither analysis nor explanation, that the decision below conflicts with a list of decisions in other circuits. Upon reading those cases, however, it is found that they all involve distinctly different considerations. *United States v. Texas Mexican Railway Co.*, 263 F. 2d 31 (CA 5) and *Commissioner v. Fifth Avenue Coach Lines*, 281 F. 2d 556 (CA 2) involve the outcome of a single contest—the inherently unpredictable all-or-nothing situation as distinguished from an aggregate of several hundred contests where the aggregate may be subject to reasonable prediction even though each single item taken separately is not.

Capital Warehouse Co. v. Commissioner, 171 F. 2d 395 (CA 8) and *Spencer, White & Prentis v. Commissioner*, 144

F. 2d 45 (CA 2) both involve deduction not of an estimate of a present liability but of an estimate of liabilities predicted to arise in the future for payment of salaries to employees to recompense them for services to be performed in the future.

Spring Canyon Coal Co. v. Commissioner, 43 F. 2d 78 (CA 10), bears a superficial resemblance to the instant case but in fact illustrates exactly what this taxpayer did *not do*. The Government admitted as much in the Court below. Spring Canyon Coal Co. attempted to set up and deduct a self insurance reserve equal to the amount of insurance premiums it would have paid had it not been a self-insurer. Such a technique illustrates perfectly the true reserve against events which may occur in the future. As a matter of fact the present taxpayer has on its books a similar true reserve account (wholly separate from the liability account here in controversy) which it has *not*, however, attempted to deduct for tax purposes. (Joint Exhibits 5-E, contained in the record certified by the Tax Court to the Court of Appeals but not printed.)

Finally, the Petition alleges conflict with the decision of the Seventh Circuit in *Streight Radio & Television, Inc. v. Commissioner*, 280 F. 2d 883, now pending on Petition for Certiorari (No. 507). The Court of Appeals, including former Chief Judge Duffy, who heard both cases, saw no conflict. The most elementary distinction is that *Streight* did not involve a deduction but an attempt to defer income and in the opinion of the Court of Appeals was governed by the decision of this Court in *Automobile Club of Michigan v. Commissioner*, 353 U. S. 180.

THE QUESTIONS IN THIS CASE ARE NOT CLOSELY RE-LATED TO OTHERS NOW PENDING BEFORE THIS COURT.

Again without explanation or analysis the Petition asserts that the question presented here is related to those involved in six cases in which petitions for certiorari have either been granted or are pending. The decisions in those cases will not control this one, or even aid in its decision. Under the applicable statutes (IRC 1954 Sec. 446, App. C., *infra*, p. 21), taxable income is to be computed in accordance with the same method of accounting the taxpayer uses for book purposes unless and only unless that method does not clearly reflect income. Only if it is determined that the method used does not reflect income, or if a change in method is sought, does the statute grant the Commissioner authority to impose a method of his own. The question presented in this and other accounting method cases (if no change of method is involved) is therefore whether the method used does or does not reflect income. Such a question is inherently factual, to be decided on the record in each case, and the decision in other cases can be helpful only where both the accounting method used and the underlying facts were essentially identical. No such comparison is possible between this case and the others pending in this Court.

Four of the cases pending do not involve deductions at all but involve instead deferral of reporting of prepaid income: *American Automobile Assn.* v. *United States*, No. 288; *New Jersey Automobile Club* v. *United States*, No. 140; *Streight Radio & Television, Inc.* v. *Commissioner*, No. 507; and *Commissioner* v. *Schlude*, No. 629. The second case in which Certiorari has already been granted, *United States* v. *Consolidated Edison Co. of New York*, No. 357, involves an important but very particularized and narrow conflict between the Court of Appeals for the Second Circuit and the Court of Claims[5] over whether accrual may ever survive payment. Since the taxpayer there did not use and the Government is not contending that it should have used a method of accounting for the contested liabilities even remotely similar to the method used by this taxpayer, nor is there any showing that it could have done so, the decision in that case must necessarily rest on totally different considerations than a decision in the instant case. Lastly, the Petition names *Fifth Avenue Coach Lines, Inc. v. Commissioner*, No. 634. As previously noted, that case involves a single and indivisible contested liability and was decided on the basis of a rule of law found inapplicable to an aggregate of a large number of separate liabilities by both of the Courts of Appeals which have had the question.

THE DECISION BELOW IS NOT A REINSTATEMENT OF REPEALED SECTION 462.

Throughout this case, both in the courts below and still now, the Government has persistently ignored and attempted to blur the distinction between a *reserve* for future liabilities and the *accrual* of the estimated amounts of liabilities already incurred, even though Treasury Regulations expressly recognize estimated accruals. (Regs. § 1.461-1 (a) (2), App. C.; *infra*, p. 23.) The Court of Appeals expressly decided that the deduction in controversy here *was* an estimated accrual and *not* a reserve. (Petition Appendix A, p. 56; 283 F. 2d 279, 286.) The Government is entitled to attempt to persuade this Court to review the decision but it is considerably less than candid when it repeatedly characterizes the deduction as a reserve as if that were an uncontested fact rather than a rejected argument. (Petition pp. 2, 4, 6, 8.)

---

5. *Consolidated Edison v. U. S.*, 135 F. Supp. 881 cert. den. 351 U. S. 909; *Chestnut Securities Co. v. U. S.*, 62 F. Supp. 574.

This insistence on mischaracterizing the deduction here as a "reserve" has had several unfortunate results. Doubtless the primary effect has been to cause petitioner to overestimate the importance and general applicability of this case. Had the Court of Appeals actually permitted this taxpayer to deduct a reserve against the cost of future events, this case might merit consideration by this Court along with some of the others now pending. Since the Court of Appeals did *not* do so, the case has no such importance.

A second result of petitioner's persistence in calling this deduction a "reserve", despite the holding and fact to the contrary, is that the case is thus made to appear to contravene the Congressional repeal of Section 462 of the 1954 Code which during its abortive life authorized deduction of a reasonable "reserve for estimated expenses." It is quite true that Section 462 would have authorized a reserve for self insurance against damages claims. *Spring Canyon Coal Co. v. Commissioner*, 43 F. 2d 78, cert. den. 284 U. S. 654, distinguished *supra*, p. 14, is doubtless a good example of the type of deduction which is not, but would have been, permitted.[6] Nothing of the sort is here involved.

THE DECISION BELOW IS CLEARLY CORRECT.

In opposing the Petition for Certiorari it would be fatuous of respondent to attempt a better defense of the decision below than it itself contains. It carefully analyzes, and for sound and explicit reasons rejects, every objection of the Government to allowance of the deduction in con-

---

6. See *Pacific Employers Insurance Co.*, 33 BTA 501. Although dealing with a statute not here applicable, the case carefully distinguishes between an unallowable reserve for losses and an allowable accrual of the aggregate estimate of liability on losses already incurred.

troversy. This taxpayer, like all taxpayers, is affirmatively required by the express wording of the applicable statute to use for tax purposes the same consistently applied recognized method of accounting which it uses in keeping its books, except only if such method does not clearly reflect its income either as a matter of fact or as a matter of law.

As a matter of fact, taxpayer's method here involved does clearly reflect its income on an annual basis, matching the expenses involved against the income of the year in the earning of which they were incurred, whereas the method sought to be imposed by the Commissioner clearly does not. Nor is there any legal exception applicable here. The exceptions relied upon by the Government have to do either with reserves against future expenses or with the impossibility of making a reasonably accurate estimate of the outcome of a specific contested claim. Neither of these has any application to the facts of this case.

In *Brown* v. *Helvering*, 291 U. S. 193, 200, this Court cited with approval *Ocean Accident & G. Corp.* v. *Commissioner*, 47 F. 2d 582, along with *United States* v. *Anderson*, 269 U. S. 422, for the proposition that a liability actually incurred during the year is a proper basis for a deduction even though the amount of the liability has not been definitely ascertained. The Court below applied identically the same rules of law as did the Second Circuit in *Ocean Accident*.

Petitioner's attempt to distinguish *Ocean Accident* by implying that the question there turned on special statutes applicable only to insurance companies demonstrates only a lack of appreciation of the question there at issue. The *kind* of deduction there was specially authorized but not the *timing* and, like the instant case, *Ocean Accident* was not concerned with *what* was deductible, but solely with *when*. The decision there did not turn on any of the special provisions applicable to insurance companies but rather on the general definition of "accrued" applicable to all taxpayers, as plainly appears from the opinion of the Second Circuit (47 F. 2d 582) as well as from the previous (reversed) opinions of the Board of Tax Appeals. (13 BTA 1058 and 16 BTA 1213.)[7] As a reading of the reversed BTA opinions will show, all of the objections which the Government raises here by focusing on the individual claims and ignoring the aggregate were raised by the Government there by focusing on the individual claims and ignoring the aggregate.

---

7. The statutes the Government cites in its petition were not enacted until after the years in controversy in *Ocean Accident*. See footnote 4, p. 8.

20

CONCLUSION.

The instant case is not in conflict with any decision of this Court or of any Court of Appeals. On the contrary it is supported in principle by the decisions of this Court and supported directly by the decision of the Second Circuit in the only reported case ever to arise on similar facts. This case involves totally different considerations than any other now pending before this Court and would require separate plenary consideration for its decision. So far as appears either on or off the record the conjunction of special circumstances which allowed this taxpayer to qualify for the deduction in controversy is extremely rare. Such a rare situation, affecting few if any other taxpayers than the present one, and totally devoid of conflict either with the decisions of this Court or among the Courts of Appeals, affords none of the ''special and important reasons'' traditionally required for the exercise of certiorari jurisdiction.

It is therefore respectfully submitted that this Petition for a Writ of Certiorari should be denied.

Respectfully submitted,

RICHARD R. TESCHNER,
ROBERT THORSEN,
WARREN W. BROWNING,
DALE L. SORDEN,
Counsel for Respondent.

April, 1961.

APPENDIX C.

___

Statutes and Regulations Involved.

INTERNAL REVENUE CODE AND REGULATIONS.

IRC 1954 Section 162.   Trade or Business Expenses.
(a)   In General.   There shall be allowed as a deduction
all the ordinary and necessary expenses paid or incurred
during the taxable year in carrying on any trade or business, * * *

IRC 1954 Section 446.   General Rule for Methods of
Accounting.   (a)   General Rule.   Taxable income shall be
computed under the method of accounting on the basis of
which the taxpayer regularly computes his income in keeping his books.

(b)   Exceptions.   If no method of accounting has been
regularly used by the taxpayer, or if the method used does
not clearly reflect income, the computation of taxable income shall be made under such method as, in the opinion
of the Secretary or his delegate, does clearly reflect income.

(c)   Permissible Methods.   Subject to the provisions of
subsections (a) and (b), a taxpayer may compute taxable
income under any of the following methods of accounting—

> (1)   the cash receipts and disbursements method;
> (2)   an accrual method;
> (3)   any other method permitted by this chapter; or
> (4)   any combination of the foregoing methods per-
>   mitted under regulations prescribed by the Secre-
>   tary or his delegate.

IRC 1954 Section 461.   General Rule for Taxable Year
of Deduction.   (a)   General Rule.   The amount of any deduction or credit allowed by this subtitle shall be taken for

the taxable year which is the proper taxable year under the method of accounting used in computing taxable income.

Regulations § 1.446-1. General Rule for Methods of Accounting. (a) General rule. (1) Section 446(a) provides that taxable income shall be computed under the method of accounting on the basis of which a taxpayer regularly computes his income in keeping his books. The term "method of accounting" includes not only the overall method of accounting of the taxpayer but also the accounting treatment of any item. Examples of such overall methods are the cash receipts and disbursements method, an accrual method, combinations of such methods, and combinations of the foregoing with various methods provided for the accounting treatment of special items. * * *

(2) It is recognized that no uniform method of accounting can be prescribed for all taxpayers. Each taxpayer shall adopt such forms and systems as are, in his judgment best suited to his needs. However, no method accounting is acceptable unless, in the opinion of the Commissioner, it clearly reflects income. A method of accounting which reflects the consistent application of generally accepted accounting principles in a particular trade or business in accordance with accepted conditions or practices in that trade or business will ordinarily be regarded as clearly reflecting income, provided all items of gross income and expense are treated consistently from year to year.

(3) Items of gross income and expenditures which are elements in the computation of taxable income need not be in the form of cash. It is sufficient that such items can be valued in terms of money. For general rules relating to the taxable year for inclusion of income and for taking deductions, see sections 451 and 461, and the regulations thereunder.

*   *   *   *   *

(b) Exceptions. (1) If the taxpayer does not regularly employ a method of accounting which clearly reflects his income, the computation of taxable income shall be made in a manner which, in the opinion of the Commissioner, does clearly reflect income.

*   *   *   *   *

(c) Permissible methods. (1) In general. Subject to the provisions of paragraphs (a) and (b) of this section, a taxpayer may compute his taxable income under any of the following methods of accounting:

*   *   *   *   *

(ii) Accrual method. Generally, under an accrual method, income is to be included for the taxable year when all the events have occurred which fix the right to receive such income and the amount thereof can be determined with reasonable accuracy. Under such a method, deductions are allowable for the taxable year in which all the events have occurred which establish the fact of the liability giving rise to such deduction and the amount thereof can be determined with reasonable accuracy. The method used by the taxpayer in determining when income is to be accounted for will be acceptable if it accords with generally recognized and accepted income tax accounting principles and is consistently used by the taxpayer from year to year. * * *

Regulations § 1.461-1. General Rule for Taxable Year of Deduction. (a) General rule—* * * (2) Taxpayer using an accrual method. Under an accrual method of accounting, an expense is deductible for the taxable year in which all the events have occurred which determine the fact of the liability and the amount thereof can be determined with reasonable accuracy. * * * While no accrual shall be made in any case in which all of the events have not occurred which fix the liability, the fact that the exact amount of the liability which has been incurred cannot be determined will not .prevent the accrual within the taxable year of such part thereof as can be computed with reasonable accuracy. For example, A renders services to B during the taxable year for which A claims $10,000. B admits the liability to A for $5,000 but contests the remainder. B may accrue only $5,000 as an expense for the taxable year in which the services were rendered. Where a deduction is properly accrued on the basis of a computation made with reasonable accuracy and the exact amount is subsequently determined in a later taxable year, the difference, if any, between such amounts shall be taken into account for the later taxable year in which such determination is made.

(3) Other factors which determine when deductions may be taken. (i) Each year's return should be complete in itself, and taxpayers shall ascertain the facts necessary to make a correct return. The expenses, liabilities, or loss of one year cannot be used to reduce the income of a subsequent year. A taxpayer may not take advantage in a return for a subsequent year of his failure to claim deductions in a prior taxable year in which such deductions should have been properly taken under his method of accounting. If a taxpayer ascertains that a deduction should have been claimed in a prior taxable year, he should, if within the period of limitation, file a claim for credit or refund of any overpayment of tax arising therefrom. Similarly, if a taxpayer ascertains that a deduction was improperly claimed in a prior taxable year, he should, if within the period of limitation, file an amended return and pay any additional tax due. However, in a going business there are certain overlapping deductions. If these overlapping items do not materially distort income, they may be included in the years in which the taxpayer consistently takes them into account.

(ii) Where there is a dispute and the entire liability is contested, judgments on account of damages for patent infringement, personal injuries or other causes, or other binding adjudications, including decisions of referees and boards of review under workmen's compensation laws, are deductions from gross income when the claim is finally adjudicated or is paid, depending upon the taxpayer's method of accounting. However, see sub-paragraph (2) of this paragraph. * * *

Lightning Source UK Ltd.
Milton Keynes UK
UKHW02f1010180718
325892UK00007B/652/P